'This is a wonderful collection of heartwarming stories of precious people. In times of much uncertainty and change, Ivan's book will re-connect you with the foundational truth that love is at the heart of things. The encounters and reflections shared so beautifully in this book will encourage you to trust that love expressed in a myriad of small moments like these are infinitely valuable and touch lives; embodying God's coming Kingdom.'

THE REVEREND LYNN GREEN
GENERAL SECRETARY – BAPTISTS TOGETHER

'Being able to reflect on the stories of encounter in our ministry is essential for every minister. It is in these encounters we see God's face and hear God's voice. Ivan King tells us the stories of some of the people who welcomed him to their lives as a friend and minister, and offers simple reflections on each story. They are stories that would resonate with what we normally encounter in ministry, and offered in gratitude, respect and affection.'

THE RIGHT REVEREND DR JOHN PERUMBALATH
BISHOP OF LIVERPOOL

Bruno

&

Other Friends

* * ♦ * *

Encounters & Reflections

Ivan Morgan King

© Ivan Morgan King 2024

The right of Ivan Morgan King to be identified as the author of the work has been asserted by him in accordance with the Copyright, Designs and Patents Act 1988.

All rights reserved. No part of this publication may be reproduced, stored in a retrieval system, or transmitted at anytime or by any means, electronic, mechanical, photocopying, recording or otherwise without the prior permission of the copyright holder. This book is sold subject to the condition that it shall not by way of trade or otherwise be circulated without the author's prior consent in any form of binding or cover other than that in which it is published.

Independently published. ISBN: 9798864733752
Author contact: parsonking@hotmail.co.uk

All Bible passages are taken from THE MESSAGE. Copyright © 1993, 1994, 1995, 1996, 2000, 2001, 2002. Used by permission of NavPress Publishing Group.

God is beyond all our pronouns: our language is just too clumsy to describe the Divine. The reader should not infer any exclusive gender for God from the use of the conventional he/him pronouns in this work.

For my family, with my love,

and in grateful memory of the

friends named in this book.

* * ◆ * *

CONTENTS

BEGINNING 3

PART ONE: ENCOUNTERS

CLAIRE 8

STUART 18

FRED AND DON 26

BRUNO 37

TUESDAY LUNCHTIME 52

JOHN RICHARDSON 62

DAVID 70

PART TWO: YOUR OWN STORY

HELEN 81

DENNIS 94

LAURA AND ASH 103

CITY CONGREGATION 110

ANNETTE AND JACK 121

BRIDGET 130

MR & MRS LANE 135

VELMA 140

PART THREE: YOU AND ME

NAMELESS 150

YOU 156

LOVE 165

NOTES, REFERENCES AND THANKS 168

* * ♦ * *

BEGINNING

Life must be lived forwards, but it can only be understood backwards.[i]

Everyone has their own collection of stories. They may remind us of early memories, happy or otherwise. Some draw upon the folklore of family, clan, nation or language. A few will be the stories that we choose to live by.

All the world's cultures tell stories. It is a distinctive of being human. We in the West are fascinated with TV soaps, celebrities and politics because we are moulded by narrative. The world's religions contribute to our stock of tales. Those to be found in the Bible have helped to shape my life and my outlook.

The great majority of all human beings who have ever lived have now been forgotten. For most, their names were only known to their families and within their villages, tribes or among their comrades in arms. Who now can tell of the differences they made? Of the days spent wrestling the earth for the right to eat or to sleep in warmth and safety? Of the jokes they shared? Or the stories of heroes they told their children around the hearth to hold the darkness at bay?

This book is a collection of encounters with ordinary people who have touched my life in extraordinary ways. They are neither famous nor powerful, but they have their very own experiences and wisdom that I want to share and celebrate. They are people who have beckoned me into their lives, as a friend, as a pastor, sometimes as a stranger or even once as an enemy. Through their stories I have glimpsed God's presence and grace amid their joys and sorrows. Though they may have passed largely unnoticed, I believe that each one has immense value as beloved children of God, as do we all.

Each tale is followed by a reflection that explores just one aspect of the Christian faith that I felt led to pursue. These reflections are not meant to be conclusive or scholarly, but rather to invite you to think more deeply about your own story and how God may speak to you through it.

I have written this collection with gratitude, respect and affection for the people whose stories I tell. I hope that by reading this book, you will be inspired by my friends' courage, faith and experience, and that you will discover new ways of seeing God at work in your own life.

I have taken care to protect their privacy and confidentiality by changing some details or names where necessary.

This is a book of my friends' stories. It is time they were heard.

Ivan King
Southend-on-Sea   Spring 2024

* * ♦ * *

Part One

ENCOUNTERS

* * ♦ * *

CLAIRE

They sat side by side in canvas chairs facing the fire-pit. Out of a sturdy white plastic carrier bag, Claire took small handfuls of dog-ends: discarded cigarette butts collected from the pavements and gutters of Southend. Most of them were burned down to within a few millimetres of the filter. A few still carried a discernible quantity of the original tobacco. With a deft movement born of long practice, Claire slit the paper binding the filter with the nail of her thumb. The redundant filter tipped over the side of her knee onto the ground, leaving a dottle of tobacco to be harvested and placed next to its brothers in a new cigarette paper resting open on her other knee. Each new roll-up might require the same movement eight to ten times. The speed and rhythm of her movements was mesmerising to watch; her focus compelling. It was like observing the devout reciting their rosary.

That afternoon, Claire and her companions had been driven through the Kent countryside, skirting opulent Tunbridge Wells, until they slipped over into East Sussex. The Co-op in Heathfield offered a final stop to check that all on board had enough Rizlas and Golden Virginia to last the weekend. Then back on to the road with its gentle rises and downward slopes. The first time finding that place, you have to follow the instructions precisely. Even after many visits, the last turning from the main road can still catch you out.

This is a rutted, stony track in spring and summer. After the last house and its barking dog, the track swings sharply to the left by the stump where Bob secreted £40 in notes just before he went missing. Then another sharp bend, this time to the right. For those who come in May, the banks here are broad green and white, heady in the sun's heat with the fragrance of wild garlic. The driver must swing to the right in front of the two tall white gateposts, placed there to ward off unwelcome visitors to what is now a wild woodland. Up the steep twisting incline to the right which grates on the gears and the suspension when the track is dry; in wet weather the unwary just skid and hope. At the top, opposite the bunkhouse, cars may be parked under the tree with the swing rope attached to the first main branch. Once, a newcomer swung there, offering an irresistible moving target for the dog who sometimes came along. He sank his teeth into prime rump!

Whoever arrives first must set the fire in the pit that will burn throughout the weekend. Having made a cradle of kindling, those skilled in woodcraft might try to bring forth sparks with knife and steel but cigarette lighters are plentiful and a couple of tea lights providentially slipped into the pocket before you leave home will do well to keep the kindling aflame, even in a breeze. Once it is alight, dried logs can be taken from the wood store. One of the tasks of the three days there will be to ensure that the store is replenished with wood freshly sawn for whoever visits next. With the fire now ablaze, the old soot-blackened kettle can sit upon the grille that lies across the bricks of the fire pit. Brewing-up is another of the rhythms of the weekend. That kettle will not grow cold over the next 48 hours.

The other must-do before the rest of the party gathers is to repair the walls of the simple ash toilet. It is just a pit over which sits a wooden box with a toilet shaped hole cut into it. By its foot stands a metal box filled with ash from previous fires, together with a ladle. It is exposed to the elements; a flimsy privacy is achieved with some willow wands standing just to shoulder height and marking a chicane entrance. A branch placed across the path alerts others that the conveniences are occupied.

Twice a year they made the journey to stay in those remote woods, along with guests from the local homeless community for perhaps their only visit outside town in twelve months. They would cook and eat together, explore the woods and talk long into the night, sat around the flames which each would take it in turn to feed from the woodpile. What faces might there be around the fire pit? Well you might think that with a half and half mixture of church and street folk the lines would be clearly drawn. Not so! Within an hour of first gathering, they are comrades together sorting the food, making tea and coffee and helping each other set up the small tents that will be their sleeping accommodation. It is impossible to predict who will be the best at telling stories or who will have the most insightful experiences to share. One or two will be skilled at crafting hot and smoky curries in the charred pots large enough to feed twenty hungry folk. There will be enough for second helpings and maybe thirds too. If the skies are clear, some may sit out tending the fire all night or sleeping in hammocks under tarps. Even in light drizzle, they sit easy in canvas chairs facing the fire, talking and laughing and joking until midnight or later. If the rain falls heavily there is a dash into a bunkhouse too small for all to sit in comfortably. At one end is an assortment of 1950s and 60s cupboards and the store of dry food for the weekend. At the other, some chairs and couple of bunks. One night, with torrential rain outside, all 20 crammed inside to eat chicken curry; street-hardened faces bright red as none was prepared to be defeated by the Scotch bonnet heat of the dinner.

Once breakfast is cooked and eaten, they restock the woodpile, using an axe or two-handed, sharp-toothed wood saw. Some set out on an exploratory expedition to see whatever there may be to find. A few will claim points of reference familiar from previous visits but there is also something about being in quite dense woodland that is disorientating. Was it not *that* tree with such a prominent branch that they passed a few minutes ago? But they follow whoever wants to lead regardless, though whether he really knows where he is going is anyone's guess.

Most of the street folk are men, though the church offers a more even blend. Some of them are young - maybe early 20s – with hard stories to tell of rejection and how they ended up on the streets. Others are older men who have simply preferred to live a life away from four walls and the kind of responsibility that enwraps most of us. Some will struggle with dependency upon alcohol or other substances but there is a fellowship of those who have lived that way which means that everyone will share their baccy and Rizlas.

After sunset, they find themselves in the darkness with all the faces illuminated by the flickering flames, toasting marshmallows on twigs. By then it is impossible to see clearly in the firelight who is from the streets and who from church. Someone has brought a guitar and everyone joins in singing songs that, given the make-up of the gathering, seem faintly bizarre. A group of mostly street-hardened men, incongruously singing the Dolly Parton song, '*Jolene*': the heartfelt pleading of one woman to another not to destroy her marriage by stealing her man.

All the while, sat on the canvas chair in front of the fire-pit, Claire spends each evening clutching and plundering the cigarette butts harvested from the streets of Southend-on-Sea and smoking the results. Burning hot on their front and with a rain-chilled back, not a few may doze there until a friend they have only just met tells another joke or story.

Staring at the flames or beyond into the clear, starlit sky they share in an experience of countless others throughout time. Wherever else God might be found that night across the wide world, there is a sense that he is at home among that gathering, sat in another canvas chair on the other side of the fire. His smiling face can be glimpsed on the far side when, for a brief moment, the wind blows the woodsmoke aside.

* * ♦ * *

Most of us have given a party at some time. Perhaps it was a birthday party, or to celebrate getting a new job. Maybe it was a picnic or a fancy-dress. I write this in the week after the road where I live was closed for a street-party to celebrate the coronation of King Charles. No matter what kind of party you give, there is much work involved. What kind of party will it be? The food and drinks will need to be bought, roping others into helping out with preparing the table. You create a playlist of the music: what would suit the atmosphere you hope for? Most importantly, you make a list of who you are going to invite and then send out the invitations.

Have you ever planned a party and sent out the invitations, but no one said they would come? How might you feel then? Angry? Sad? Hurt?

There was once a man who threw a great dinner party and invited many. When it was time for dinner, he sent out his servant to the invited guests, saying, 'Come on in; the food's on the table.' Then they all began to beg off, one after another making excuses. The first said, 'I bought a piece of property and need to look it over. Send my regrets.' Another said, 'I just bought five teams of oxen, and I really need to check them out. Send my regrets.' And yet another said, 'I just got married and need to get home to my wife.' The servant went back and told the master what had happened. He was outraged and told the servant, 'Quickly, get out into the city streets and alleys. Collect all who look like they need a square meal, all the misfits and homeless and down-and-out you can lay your hands on and bring them here.

The servant reported back, 'Master, I did what you commanded— and there's still room.' The master said, 'Then go to the country roads. Whoever you find, drag them in. I want my house full! Luke 14: 16-23

Jesus once told his listeners about a man who wanted to throw a party. It was going to be a huge celebration. But then the excuses started coming in thick and fast. The reasons people gave for being too busy to come to the celebration seemed sensible enough. Who wants to break into their honeymoon for a social obligation? Or take time out from sorting out the new house you've just bought? None of the people he had invited were willing to come to the party. They were just too focussed on their own business – and busy-ness.

The host was terribly upset and hurt, so he told his servants to go out into the streets and invite everyone they saw to come to his celebration. It didn't matter if they were friends or strangers; good or bad people. He just wanted his house to be full of people who would celebrate, eat, drink and be welcomed as honoured guests, enjoying themselves and sharing the celebration, both with him and with one another.

In this story Jesus told, those invited see the invitation as a nuisance. One went to his workplace, another to his home. There is no hint here of any of the invitees being bad people. Don't miss the point - these are responsible, busy people in the everyday working world. They are simply so consumed with the 'busy-ness' of their schedules that nothing can break through. How often do we ignore or reject a kind invitation that comes unexpectedly, because we are too busy with our own plans?

The host is frustrated that people offer excuses why they cannot come to his party. So he sends out his workers to the alleys and backstreets of life, to the people everyone looks down upon, those from the gutters and pavements and places where nice people won't go, to bring them into the banquet. There are to be no excuses. He tells his team to go and drag people in, to feast, drink and celebrate with him. He is determined that his house will be full.

Sometimes in life you catch a glimpse of what this story hints at. I did at our fireside gathering, in the shared food, stories and songs. We may be surprised at the people sat either side of us at the celebration – people who started out as strangers. They may be 'awkward' people with whom we feel uncomfortable (and perhaps they with us, too). Yet, strangest of all, we also have been invited and have been given the grace to overcome the too-ready excuses of shyness or busy-ness.

We sometimes talk of places as godforsaken, don't we? I think we also dismiss some people as being beyond both the loving reach of God and also beyond acceptance as fellow human beings. Perhaps we think of ourselves that way. Yet I believe that God moves into all and every neighbourhood, making each one where he chooses to live. Christians believe there will come a time when he does this finally and forever. The Bible hints that the whole of creation stands on tiptoe eagerly awaiting the changes that God will bring about on that day. For the God who chose to be born in flesh and became like us has declared that he is making his home among us. Among us, right now. In Southend-on-Sea, or in a wild wood in Sussex or wherever we are.

I used to think that when Jesus gave his followers the task of going to share the good news of God's love with all kinds of people, dipping them in water as a sign of a new beginning for their life, that meant that he was giving the church a task to undertake while he himself would be absent. I no longer believe that. We are called to go and share his good news with all people simply because God is out there doing that already. He has chosen to be here: present among us.

If we went looking for God in Southend-on-Sea today, where might we expect to find him? Where would you hope to glimpse God at work in your home neighbourhood? Well I hope that we might find him in many churches. But that is not the only place where the always-present God has chosen to make his home among us. I would expect to glimpse Jesus in the bar opposite the church, concerned to befriend and nurture people there who might not always be welcomed in church, seeking their love and offering companionship. For God did not send his Son into the world to condemn anyone but to bring all into his home for a feast.

I would expect to find Jesus on Ambleside Avenue, with the streetwalkers, the kerb-crawlers and the weed-sellers. I would hope to see Jesus on the top of the tower blocks or by the railways lines as desperate people consider ending their lives. I would hope to find Jesus - who is born into our world to reclaim it from despair and brokenness - in the nightclubs and in the houses where isolated people live; with anxious commuters worrying about their jobs and parents scared for their children's future.

So, sitting in the company of others and hearing the stories written here, maybe across the fire and through the smoke, we too may catch a glimpse of him. Maybe he is sat right next to us already. In which case, why not risk striking up a conversation with him?

* * ♦ * *

STUART

Every minister, priest and community worker knows Stuart or someone like him. He was about 35 and drawn to church as one of the few places of welcome for someone who most people found too awkward or too threatening. I suppose he should be described as having an alcohol dependency but labels are too easy; too quick to condemn and separate. Like many of his friends, when sober he was friendly but the bottle had eroded his inhibitions.

What was very clear was that he knew nothing of the refined, unspoken but well-understood culture of a suburban Baptist church. He would always come and sit in the front row: something that immediately set him apart from everyone else. The church used the quaint formula of inviting the congregation to 'gather' around the Lord's Table for communion: requiring movement of the soul, not the feet. In those days they tended to serve the bread and cup in the pews, so no one was expecting anyone actually to move. Then Stuart came and sat on one of the wooden 'thrones' behind the communion table, which seemed natural enough to him but caused some ripples of disquiet for others. Oh dear. Here was real life breaking in on tradition.

Stuart visited the church when he needed help. Often the help he sought was financial rather than friendship or food or warmth. For that reason he was often disappointed.

There is one day that springs to mind whenever I think about Stuart. In the south London of my youth, we might have used a vulgar phrase to describe how utterly drunk Stuart was as he made his way into the church that day. It was a Saturday and we were going to have some baptisms the following morning. If you have never observed a baptism in a Baptist church, you may not know that we immerse the candidate fully in a pool of water which, in most cases, is cleverly concealed under the floor at the front of the congregation. It wasn't just a question of running a big bath of around 3 cubic metres of water. For this was heated by portable immersion heaters – like giant springs. These had to be plugged into an ancient and temperamental wall socket, on a circuit restricted to that purpose alone. Well one day, the usual team who took care of these things were away so the task of preparation fell to me. While I was trying to get my head around taping down splash-proof matting and arranging the barriers so that no one could slip into the pool, I had unwisely left the front door unlocked. Then into the church came Stuart.

He and I were alone in the sanctuary. All of my attention was focussed upon making sure the church did not get flooded or that anyone should risk electrocution. I looked up at one point and there was Stuart sat in a pew on the right-hand side of the church. Having explained that I needed to concentrate on the tasks at hand, I told Stuart that he was really welcome to stay and watch me work and, of course, to return for the celebration the following morning.

So he sat and watched. He was drunk, sure, but not in a way that presented immediate problems. It was only afterwards that I realised that he must have come into the church to borrow money to buy some papers for making roll-up cigarettes, as he tried to use pages from St Matthew's gospel in the pew Bibles. Then, all at once he was gone; I did not notice his quiet departure.

It was about 30 minutes after that that I discovered that my jacket, my wallet and my mobile phone had gone too. Fortunately, my own keys and the enormous bunch of church keys were still to be found. I am notoriously scatter-brained about where I have left things and so it took me quite some time to satisfy myself that the coat, the wallet and phone had indeed gone and that Stuart was the most likely agent of their disappearance. By now very irritated, I put a stop on the cards; received a crime reference number from the police and fumed at the inconvenience of it all. Before the cards were stopped by the bank, they had already been traded and used by someone to buy £200 worth of who knows what?

The following morning I was in church early preparing for that morning's service. The congregation – always more numerous for a baptism – were gathering and the sanctuary had the welcome feel of a live event about to unfold. Then Stuart walked in, wearing my leather jacket. A good friend, a talented amateur boxer named Bruno, saw the look on my face before I managed to get across the room and stood by in case there was trouble but there was none, thankfully. Stuart had sobered up. He remembered selling the credit cards and the phone in the park after leaving the church, following which he had become even more drunk.

The jacket and mobile were both second-hand. The cards were quickly stopped and replaced. But this man had now come to his senses. He felt broken and had come to church to ask to be forgiven.

When did we first forget that church is for broken people? When did we start to think that a life following Jesus is for people who are respectable, sorted and OK?

He told his next story to some who were complacently pleased with themselves over their moral performance and looked down their noses at the common people: "Two men went up to the Temple to pray, one a Pharisee, the other a tax man. The Pharisee posed and prayed like this: 'Oh, God, I thank you that I am not like other people—robbers, crooks, adulterers, or, heaven forbid, like this tax man. I fast twice a week and give away ten percent on all my income.'

Meanwhile the tax man, slumped in the shadows, his face in his hands, not daring to look up, said, 'God, give mercy. Forgive me, a sinner.'

Jesus commented, "This tax man, not the other, went home made right with God. If you walk around with your nose in the air, you're going to end up flat on your face, but if you're content to be simply yourself, you will become more than yourself." Luke 18: 9-14

In this story Jesus tells, two men go to worship God. The first is a Pharisee: a member of a sect among Jews who believed in rigorous obedience to the Law of Moses. He is a successful man who is respected by his fellow worshippers. He is familiar with the patterns of worship. Above all, he is confident because he knows that he has done everything expected of him. It is upon this same confidence and his manner of life that he now prays openly and noisily to God, so that everyone there notices his devotion and approves.

The other is not a good man. Everyone else going to the service that day is astonished to see him there. They despise him. This man collaborates with the hated enemy occupiers of their homeland. He fleeces people of their hard-earned money, turning over the bulk of it to those who have invaded their country while keeping a good margin for himself. He is ill-at-ease with worship, for he has not been for so long. He is far from confident. In fact, he is quite literally beating himself up, smashing his hands against his chest.

Which of these two people truly encountered and engaged with God in that place of worship?

The parables of Jesus are not moralising tales, with easy lessons to learn and apply. They were intended to make those who heard them laugh, cry or become enraged by their exaggeration, oddness, pain or unfairness. So how do you feel having heard this story?

When did you first forget that church is for broken people, like Stuart? When did you start to think that the life of faith is for people who think they are already sorted? If someone like Stuart came to join your church, what would it be like for him? What is there, in your time of worship, that would relieve this man of his burdens and enable him to encounter the love of God? What in all your familiar words might welcome and accept him as he is?

In the same way, I would want to ask what there is in church services that meets us in the reality of our daily life? For, unless you are completely different to me, many of us are like Eleanor Rigby, 'wearing the face that we keep in a jar by the door' kept just for meeting others and especially for Sunday at church.

What I mean is this. Among the neighbours who live around us will be people who are experiencing loneliness, illness or the fear of illness, physical, mental or emotional pain, addiction to internet pornography, struggles with identity, strain in family relationships, a boss who behaves hatefully, those who experience daily difficulty in making ends meet or who are hip-deep in anger, depression or anxiety. Perhaps you recognise some of this in yourself?

So many of us are good at concealing all of this. The person living in the flat above yours could be facing their darkest despair or a major breakdown and you wouldn't know from their smile. On the occasions that people do show their burdens by their behaviour or their appearance, we often find them an embarrassment.

What is true for others is often also true for us – people of faith. So often we leave our burdens at the church door for an hour, then collect them again as we leave. So when did we first forget that church is for broken people? When did we start to think that we are not in need of repair?

Now please understand that I am not criticising you, your faith, your worshipping community or your life. I am not trying to undermine anything. I simply ask you to reflect. How much of what we as followers of Jesus do pays attention to the purpose of church in modelling what life is like when things are done God's way? John, in his first letter in the New Testament, says this:

Whoever claims to love God yet hates a brother or sister is a liar. For whoever does not love their brother and sister, whom they have seen, cannot love God, whom they have not seen. And he has given us this command: Anyone who loves God must also love their brother and sister.' 1 John 4:19-21

To hate someone is nothing really to do with clenching our fists and declaring someone to be your enemy. It is when we are so consumed with our ways that we become recklessly indifferent to the needs of other people. It is what the first man did in the story Jesus told. He glanced at God; looked with contempt on his fellow man but then focused his attention firmly upon himself. He thought that was what 'worship' was.

If you have faith and really want to know how much you love God, ask yourself how much you love the person you dislike the most or find most difficult to deal with. That is a good measure. On the other hand, if you are well aware of how messy your life is and how no self-help manual alone will fix what is broken, how about taking the path of the second man in the story? Give God your mistakes and messiness and ask for a fresh start.

* * ♦ * *

FRED AND DON

20 Walton Road
Sidcup
Kent

                      897904 Bdr King D.
            HQ 470/97 (KY) Field Regt
                          Royal Artillery
                                    C.M.F.

        8th May 1945

Dear Don,

'Unarm! The long day's work is done.' You have finished the job that we left unfinished in 1918. The foul beast is in the dust, damned and done for. Justice has been done. It is difficult to write without emotion. Now as the last minutes of the day are slipping away, I strive to marshal my rambling thoughts in an effort to tell you what it is like here and what we think. It makes me wish that I could hold back time, hold this golden hour long enough to give me time to reflect before it reels on into eternity. But all I get is a rush of confused thoughts and memories.

I am not ashamed to admit that uppermost is the thought 'Don is safe.' As I told you, alone in the family I had played this bloody game of war. Alone I knew something of what you were going into and so, alone, in thought and spirit, I have followed you till the bugles made ceasefire. Your gallant assertions that you were 'never in danger' never deceived me, though they served their purpose in easing mother's mind. Today and tomorrow are holidays - today we have been to Stanley and Gladys at Petts Wood and had real champagne (Moet 1921) and the only toast was you and all those that have made today possible.

Tomorrow I go to work voluntarily, to help to pay repatriated prisoners of war. It's the least I can do. Outside it looks and sounds like an air raid. Big fires are burning, search lights are streaming into the night, planes are wheeling overhead, sirens are going and there is a fluttering around such as was made during air raids by the silver strips the Germans used to drop to defeat radio-location. But the fires are bonfires, the search lights are only dancing a joyful fandango all over the skies, the planes are lit up and are rolling over in irrepressible fun, the sirens are from ships and factories and, as one peers through the dark, one can see countless flags making that quiet fluttering. Lights stream from uncurtained windows and rockets, not those that we have grown used to, shoot up and burst in sparkling colours. For this men women and children have suffered and endured, fought and worked, bled and died. The world is a cleaner place tonight. No more crouching in shelters, no more wailing sirens, no more wondering if the house and Dorcas will still be there on my return, no more wondering if Don will still get through safely. For you as for us, total war has been over some while. The achievements of the army under Alexander are beyond any praise I could muster. He never talked, he never publicised, he didn't order a salvo of guns but he broke the heart of the finest army Germany had got. As I warned you, a grateful country is quite likely to forget to thank you but the measure of what you have done is known best to you. That is your reward, that and the fact that I sit here in this quiet room, at ease, mentally and physically, because of what you, and such as you, have done. There are more things for which thanks is an insult. This is one of them but only because words are such empty vessels an adequate hour.

Dorcas has gone to bed. I'm just going to have a little drink all by myself and drink to those who had endured the days, the weeks, the months, the years, to those who have saved us, who saved the world, the common soldier, who took the place of the broken army that I had spent my life with, that kept alight the torch that fell from its dying hands.

God bless you. Fred

* * ♦ * *

Mary came to where Jesus was waiting and fell at his feet, saying, "Master, if only you had been here, my brother would not have died." When Jesus saw her sobbing and the Jews with her sobbing, a deep anger welled up within him. He said, "Where did you put him?" "Master, come and see," they said. Now Jesus wept. John 11: 32-35

In December 1915, a Christmas letter from his

family was received by Fred, a 20-year old sergeant serving in the trenches of northern France. It contained much welcome news from the family home, a terraced house in East Dulwich but then, as his parents signed off the letter with their love, they included the mysterious line: "Your brother Don sends his love." Don was the sixth child of the family in which Fred was the eldest half-brother – and this was the first he had heard of the arrival of a new sibling.

In 2015, Don - my late father - would have celebrated his 100th birthday. Although he died when I was just into my twenties, I think of him often. When I was a child I used to think that he and I were completely dissimilar. Of course, our life experiences were radically different. Yet I see aspects of my father now in my reactions and my character and I also have the surprise of catching glimpses of him in my son, the grandson whom he never met, who has inherited his physique and something of his humour and good nature. I miss him very much.

Uncle Fred was ancient when I knew him. He stayed on in the army after the armistice in 1918 and finished his military career with the rank of major. He and his wife, my aunt Dorcas, had travelled to exotic places around the world with the army but then retired to a bungalow on the coast in Kent, where we would visit once a year for quite a formal afternoon tea. Before the meal, Uncle Fred would tell many military stories, including some that – charitably – might have become embellished in the half-century then since the end of WW1.

It was only much later that we found, in my parents' papers, the letter that Fred had written his youngest brother on VE (Victory in Europe) Day in 1945, when his brother Don was serving in Italy, having been in the North African and Sicilian campaigns as a Desert Rat. Though phrased in the language of the times and written by someone who had seen and been shaped by the horrors of trench warfare, gas-attacks and the carnage of WW1, the deep brotherly concern and relief at the end of hostilities carries still across the 80 years since the letter was written on that historic night.

Neither Fred nor Don claimed to be religious in their approach to life. But both had been in many situations when their lives were under imminent threat and they were confronted by the death, injury, disfigurement and suffering of comrades, civilians, communities and landscapes. Although Fred mentions God in his letter, I don't know whether he had any personal faith or was simply calling upon the prevalent religion of his time and military experience.

'In the midst of life, we are in death' according to the burial service in the Book of Common Prayer. When comforting a friend who had lost her husband, the late Queen Elizabeth, the Queen Mother was asked if grieving got any better with the passage of time. She replied: 'It doesn't get any better but you get better at it.' That is my experience. Perhaps it is the experience of some of you reading this now, for almost all of us have had to cope with loss and grief. For other people, events such as the annual Remembrance Sunday show that grief can be carried for a very long time.

What help does faith in God offer us as we confront the reality of death? The Old Testament supplies us many examples of how God's people in ancient times coped with fear, grief, loss and death. The psalms provide us with many laments, including those echoed by Jesus Himself: *'My God, My God, why have you forsaken me?'*

Well, the event we read above from the life of Jesus is about death and grief in the midst of life; and the place of faith and hope in such times. Lazarus, Martha and Mary lived close to Jerusalem. They were followers and close friends of Jesus. When Jesus came to Jerusalem he stayed with them. Apart from that we know little about them: they seem to have been independent, without parents in the picture; they must have been financially comfortable, since they had a house large enough to cater for groups of people like those who followed Jesus.

On one of Jesus' visits, Martha got annoyed by the unequal share of housework she had to do while Mary, whom she thought should have been sharing the load, sat listening to Jesus talk. Martha complained to Jesus, but he seemed unconcerned, taking Mary's side. Don't worry so much about practical things, he said - concentrate on what is most important.

This time, when Jesus was absent, Lazarus became gravely ill. Then he got worse, and the two women sent for Jesus. Come and cure our brother, they begged. Jesus received the message but he put off coming for two days. Why? Jesus clearly loved this man as a friend. Their home was just a short stroll from Jerusalem. Yet Jesus stays on in the city when a minimal effort could have brought his miraculous healing. The disciples – bless them – are typically slow to grasp the seriousness of Lazarus' condition.

Then Lazarus dies. For all the miracles worked by Jesus, people still died in Judea in the years of his ministry. People still suffered disabilities; there was still poverty and injustice and the land remained under enemy occupation. The presence of the Son of God does not remove us from the ills of the human condition. For that reason I cannot sing certain lines in popular worship songs that suggest that in his presence our problems disappear. I understand the sentiment but to me such words are high-sounding nonsense, at risk of disrespecting and diminishing the pain of others who do not receive immediate relief from the crushing pressures they face.

When Jesus eventually arrived, Martha rushes out to meet him. She reproached Jesus bitterly - if you'd only come sooner, he wouldn't have died, she said. She berates her friend for delaying and we cannot miss her tone of disappointment. Then, in a flash of intuition, she called him something extraordinary: the Messiah, Son of

God. Later in John's gospel, Peter – and then Thomas – also are led through circumstances to acclaim Jesus but Martha gets there first. Mary, who in the previous story had earned Jesus' praise for prioritizing time listening to him above the chores of everyday life, is here distraught.

As a pastor, I have comforted grieving people. At such times, the questions all seem to begin with 'Why?' Why me? Why did this happen? Why do such bad things happen, even to good people? Why did God allow that to happen?

Having thought about the disciples, Martha and Mary, now we look at Jesus, who is also crying. Why? (There's that word again). Why is Jesus weeping? Some commentators suggest that surely, as the Son of God, he knew that Lazarus would be fine in the end – so why weep? Yet this man, Jesus, was fully human. He did not know all things. Others suggest that it only began to dawn on Jesus at that point – when confronted with the death of his friend – about the awful process of dying and the death that he anticipated would await him shortly. Let's not forget that John's gospel is the gospel of significance. Every act and story in this gospel is drenched in meaning.

Jesus wept because he loved his friend, who is now dead. Jesus wept because of his own grief and because his friends, Martha and Mary, were now experiencing the desperate loss and pain that comes when death robs us of those we love. Jesus wept because grief is the price that we pay for having loved.

And what of poor Lazarus? Let's take a moment to place ourselves in his position. What might he have thought, as he became ill, then worsened? His friend the healer is just a short walk away, so why hasn't he come? His family have sent word, but no one arrives. Then the loss of hope as, for him, time runs out. Then – what? Nothingness? Or a glimpse of paradise? Until, days after he died, the shock of resurrection and a powerful voice summoning him back to earthly life. He is restored to family and friends and becomes the first to taste that even death cannot separate us from the love of God found in Christ.

Yet Lazarus died again. How long did he have? We are not told. I think his restored life might have been quite problematic. There are always seekers after the supernatural and they would have shown an unhealthy interest in him. Some would have thought him part of a conspiracy to deceive. He would have been a political and religious embarrassment. And how do you relate then to your friend who has so publicly transformed your very existence?

At the heart of this passage is this. *Jesus says to Martha: 'I am the resurrection and the life. The one who believes in me will live, even though they die; and whoever lives by believing in me will never die. Do you believe this?' 'Yes, Lord,' she replied, 'I believe that you are the Messiah, the Son of God, who is to come into the world.' John 11:27*

The words that Jesus proclaims to Martha invite us not to be glib or to wear a shallow smile in the face of grief and pain. Perhaps like you, in times of loss I have suffered from the bright cheerfulness of Christians who would do better to stand weeping, like our Master, rather than offering trite religious platitudes that masquerade as faith.

Jesus doesn't offer us an easy way out. Like Lazarus, one day we will all face death first-hand. Jesus does not tell us that we can avoid death or grief. But he offers us the solid hope that lies on the far side of that most human experience. And the one who stands and weeps at the grave of his friend is the one who stands beside us as we face all that life can throw at us. He came into the world, born as one of us, entering our condition – our frailty, our hopelessness and the apparent finality of the death that awaits us. He goes on standing beside us, sharing our tears and offering us hope.

When grief has knocked us down, sometimes we experience the presence of Christ in the touch of a hand, or a hug, or a meal cooked and brought round or by someone looking at our treasured photographs with us. Christ may use the community of faith to show his care.

When we meet together, do we make allowance for grief and loss in our worship? For lament? We sometimes fall into the trap of thinking that we must leave our feelings and the reality of life at the church door when we come to worship. Or that we must be unremittingly cheerful. What nonsense! The psalmists knew, often better than us, that worship consists in bringing the whole of life before God.

Fred and Don saw a great deal of death at first hand. Who knows how many they themselves killed, with rifle, bayonet, Tommy gun or artillery shells? They felt the fear of death and of loss too. They lived with the aftermath of the sights they had seen and the people they had lost. Their families lived in fearfulness about their safety across two world wars. Today, we are fortunate to be greatly sheltered from such. Which is why I find Remembrance Day to be a useful reminder to pay attention. It is a useful point in our church calendar to remember, to reflect and in thankfulness to recall the lives now past that have touched ours. To hand over, once again, those we have loved and who have died into God's tender care.

We do so understanding that there is no safer place than in the hands of the God who firstly imagined our loved ones and then called them into existence. He has done the same for us. He is the always-with-us God, who stands with us and shares our tears. His declaration that he is the resurrection and the life is matched by a demonstration of power in the gift of new life to Lazarus. So let us share life together with its joys and its sorrows, bringing them both in our worship of God. Let that worship include thanksgiving and lament as we gather round the Jesus of both tears and solid hope.

* * ♦ * *

BRUNO

For I am convinced that neither death nor life, neither angels nor demons neither the present nor the future, nor any powers, neither height nor depth, nor anything else in all creation, will be able to separate us from the love of God that is in Christ Jesus our Lord. Romans 8:38-39

Remember, this is *not* a funeral.

Funerals are for those who have reached the end of their life. We Christians instead hold services of celebration and thanks to God. We meet, we worship, in the name of Christ, the One who died and is risen. We proclaim that Christ died for us, and that Christ lives, and that because Christ lives, no one is beyond redemption. We neither deny death nor diminish the pain of it, but we insist that love is stronger.

Today in our sadness at Bruno's passing we shout aloud in defiance that Bruno was, is, and always will be a beloved child of God. Scattering the darkness, this man's life blazed with the dazzling light of Christ and when we see him again, he will shine like the sun in his Father's presence.

Bruno first became our friend just before the

millennium year. In those days we had the first of several Congolese congregations sharing the church premises with us. Boisterous, their exuberance in worship rang loudly in heaven's ears but, sadly, just as noisily in the homes of our neighbours in Wellesley Road. For that reason they had to move on to other premises. But Bruno stayed.

A young Congolese man, then aged around 20; his first languages were Lingala and French. He stayed and dug himself into the spiritual earth of this church and started putting down roots. And so, very quickly, Bruno became family.

Were we aware of the process of his becoming part of us, and us joining in his life? I don't think so. My recollection is that Sunday morning worship and Bruno simply fitted together naturally. A Sunday morning without Bruno could seem a little lifeless.

He dressed joyously but that was exactly right, for he had an exuberant faith. One thing I cherish from those years was the weekly opportunity for anyone to come forward and inspire us by their appreciation of what God was doing in their life. Or to share their sorrows, so that they became common property to us all. On so many Sundays Bruno would come to the front both to encourage us and to challenge us to greater faith. His faith didn't get stuck at the thinking stage; it went on to dare and to try. Coming from most other people the content and tone of Bruno's exhortations might have created some resentment. But those of us who loved this man knew that he spoke with integrity, so his words didn't jar; they carried the weight of lived experience and deep love.

On one occasion, a previous minister - an old friend of the church - came to be guest speaker and, during the service, Bruno brought a word of challenge. The minister said to some of us afterwards: 'Treasure that man!' And treasure him we did. We listened to and valued this brother who, for all the boldness of his public words, lived humbly and never sought the spotlight for himself.

God gave our brother two marvellous gifts and, through him, lent them also to us. He had a depth of faith that shot through his prayers. His prayers were solid in their trust in God. Given the experiences he had undergone, that was remarkable.

The other gift he had was that of insight. During his time here, Bruno would quietly tell me what he believed God had revealed to him in his prayers. These were quite staggering insights into spiritual needs that, at times, could not possibly have been known to any but the individuals themselves. After 2007, Bruno would occasionally phone me from his new home near Brazzaville – at tremendous cost for someone who most of the time had no work – and urge me to speak to…. well, whoever. He had been praying for them and felt God stirring his mind, revealing something that would affirm or strengthen them. Even though he was 4,000 miles away and cut off from us by distance, circumstance, culture and poverty, he continued to exercise this great gift. He did so humbly. Though we were apart, he still thought of us as family.

Bruno had a very wide range of interests. He was a light heavyweight amateur boxer and some of you, I know, had the opportunity to see him in the ring. There was at least one occasion when I (whom God has not equipped to be a pugilist) was grateful to have the reassuring presence of a light heavyweight boxer at my side in a tense situation. He loved driving and dancing and shared with friends a love of country and western music.

Our friend's father had been in the employment of the then President of the Republic of Congo. He was unimportant politically but, simply because of his connections, he was brutally murdered. We thank God that Bruno didn't witness this hateful event but he was warned to flee immediately or face the same fate. So he fled. Most of you won't know this but Bruno left close members of his family behind, and from whom he cut off contact, when he left the country. I am sure this was for their protection. For most of us, having to leave those most dear with the prospect that you might never see them again would be unbearable. It was another burden that he carried without complaining.

He claimed asylum in this country. Of all the places in the world, he came to Ilford. He supported himself financially by working as a dustman for Barking & Dagenham Council, an employment in which he excelled. He featured with his colleagues in a training DVD that he was very proud of and I have seen the many work-related certificates he gained. He was not a drain on the public purse. He worked hard. He was a model citizen.

He pursued his asylum case until he had exhausted all appeals, although he bore in his body the proofs of persecution. It would be self-indulgent to vent our frustration with the immigration authorities at their refusal to accept his claims. They have an unenviable task and they are also children of God, as fallible as the rest of us. Yet, while Bruno didn't carry his hurts and fears openly, I know that he had a compelling case to remain here. Our country has lost a hard worker and an honest and upright contributor to the common good. Our nation is the poorer, in so many ways, for the way it handled his case and many others too.

On behalf of those who loved him, thank-you to those who offered to fund his bail and any further legal interventions. Some of us were there to hear the immigration appeals judge lament that he wished his decision could go in favour of a man so evidently loved by the community in which he lived and worked. It was not to be.

A few of us managed to get into the detention centre near Cambridge and to take his instructions for disposal of his property.

When Bruno was deported in February 2007,

despite all appeals and all steps to prevent it, he could have lost hope. It is testament to our brother that he didn't, despite the shock of sudden temperature changes, malaria, power shortages and the chronic lack of work and money. He moved in with his brother's family, found a church and just got on with life. After a while he made a new friend to whom he became engaged – a woman whose faith in Christ matched his. He found occasional work as a driver.

We are all wondering about the events that brought us here today. Like many of you, I am not convinced by the explanation we have been given. But it may be that what we have heard is true. That death came into Bruno's life pretending to be the only answer to his troubles. That Bruno thought death could be a friend.

What gives me strong hope for today is that the blood of Christ covers all of life's events. When Bruno first put his faith in Christ, then all his mistakes and wrongdoing, past and future, were forgiven. And nothing, *nothing* can separate us from the love of God in Jesus Christ.

Nothing, not even death.

Are we sad to be here today? Yes, of course. We weep together and that is right. But this is not the end of the story. Because of the faith in Christ that this man held to, we can say that Bruno will now rest in peace and rise in glory. However brightly he sometimes sparkled among us here, we trust everlasting light now shines upon him. He is safe in the company of heaven.

As for us, let us weep indeed, let us mourn and miss, but not as those who have no hope. For when Christians gather to say farewell to someone so-loved, we mix our tears with thanks to God.

Thank-you for this man, his life, his example and the privilege of sharing life's journey with him for 12 years. Thank-you for the ways in which God touched his life and ours. Let us leave here today, more than ever resolved to treasure each other. God gives us one another as precious gifts, to love, to enjoy and to work with until we and Bruno are together again in the presence of God.

We give thanks for the life of Jean Bruno Mbou, borrowing words from Psalm 136:

God remembered us when we were down,

His love never fails.
Rescued us from the trampling boot,

His love never fails.
Takes care of everyone in time of need.

His love never fails.
Thank God, who did it all!

His love never fails! Amen

* * ♦ * *

Why? Why has this happened? Why do bad things happen to good people? Why did God allow Bruno to be rescued from the persecution that threatened him in the Republic of Congo only, later, to be sent back there to die?

About that time some people came up and told him about the Galileans Pilate had killed while they were at worship, mixing their blood with the blood of the sacrifices on the altar. Jesus responded, 'Do you think those murdered Galileans were worse sinners than all other Galileans? Not at all. Unless you turn to God, you, too, will die. And those eighteen in Jerusalem the other day, the ones crushed and killed when the Tower of Siloam collapsed and fell on them, do you think they were worse citizens than all other Jerusalemites? Not at all. Unless you turn to God, you, too, will die.' Luke 13: 1-5

Jesus is talking to a crowd when people ask him about what was, for them, a recent and painful situation. What about those Galileans who got religious fervour when they saw the Roman symbols in the temple? The Roman governor sent in the troops who slaughtered them, spilling those worshippers' blood in what was the holiest place in the land. How could God allow this to happen? Aside from the shock, the anger and the blasphemy of invaders entering the temple, the question is: where is God when all this is happening?

Jesus then raises another incident. A building had collapsed and 18 people had been killed. Apparently innocent people dying for seemingly no reason. And the first point that Jesus makes here is that none of those who died were more deserving of death than anyone else. God had not singled them out.

Why did this happen to him or to her? Why is this happening to me? And what kind of God would *make* this happen or *allow* it to happen? Don't you ever wonder? I do.

I am aware of the danger of treading too heavily on ground that may be painful. Yet the search for truth and meaning is sometimes painful. If we only just talk about the pleasant aspects of life we may miss the truth. Faith then just becomes another distraction from reality.

Alongside the many blessings we have in life, there are darker times. People die. They get cancer. They lose their jobs. They don't have enough money to live well. People have faced misfortune for thousands of years of recorded history. There are wars. Sadly, we see it today in Ukraine.

Some of those who have died behaved in an obviously evil way. Mostly they were ordinary people like you and me. Did they deserve their fate? Jesus makes the point that we must not assume that people who face misfortunes are being punished. For much of human history, people thought that God punishes the wicked and rewards those who lived morally good lives. When misfortune fell on someone, you could be sure the victim 'had it coming to him.'

Yet the same people who believe that the misfortunes of life are God's punishment believe (as I do) that all of us are imperfect, not living up to our own standards or to God's. So why would God give one person a heart attack and not another, if such things are a punishment for our brokenness or imperfection?

So much of life is a mystery and we don't get to see, know or understand why bad things happen as they do. St Paul said:

"For now we see through a mirror dimly, but then we shall see face to face; right now I know only in part, but then I shall understand fully, even as I have been fully understood." 1 Corinthians 13:12

People of faith try to live with hope regardless of the circumstances. As a Christian, I try to draw my understanding from the Bible. Yet the Bible shows an evolving understanding of God and how and why he acts. These understandings are mediated through the humanity of the various writers. For example, in the Psalms we often find the writers demanding that God should come and hurt their enemies, to repay them in-kind for the hurt done to innocent and upright people. Yet I cannot imagine Jesus praying for the same.

Here's my take on the topic. You may not agree with me – indeed I am open to challenge. At least it is a starting point…

Bad stuff happens to us all. God does not send cancer or cause terrible accidents. He does not decide that Miss X will be made redundant. He doesn't cause Mr Y to drink alcohol before he drives his car, leaving someone with life-changing injuries.

Lots of people will quote Old Testament passages that appear to show a direct link between people doing evil and their deserved punishment by God. But it is not that straightforward. Even the best, most godly of the kings we find in the Old Testament may have done everything right but this did not guarantee them a long life. King Josiah is described in the Bible as a righteous king who "walked in all the way of David his father, and turned not aside to the right hand or to the left." Yet he died after being wounded in battle aged just 39.

All of the great 'heroes' of the Old Testament were as flawed as you and me. And then there's also this curious Old Testament passage:

> *I took another walk around the neighbourhood and realized that on this earth as it is—*
>
> *The race is not always to the swift,*
> *Nor the battle to the strong,*
> *Nor satisfaction to the wise,*
> *Nor riches to the smart,*
> *Nor grace to the learned.*
> *Sooner or later bad luck hits us all.* Ecclesiastes 9:11

'Bad luck!' In other words, it is possible that God does not micro-manage his creation – and our fate - in the way we want. I would like a God who puts on his red cape and shorts and flies faster than a speeding bullet, leaping tall buildings at one bound. In churches, many of our modern worship songs emphasise the great power of

God – and we are disappointed when he does not always use that power to save people from harm.

Instead, he has chosen to be incarnate: to be born among us as a human being. Like us he experiences the joys, the mundane, the pain and also the suffering. He offers us strength and courage *within* a situation, not necessarily escape *from* it. And time and chance overtake us all… It is our common experience of being human, even if the details vary from person to person.

I must challenge in myself the idea that if I do all the 'right things': pray, read the Bible, go to church, give money and time to charities, stay away from behaving in selfish and hurtful ways and instead do nice things for others, then shouldn't I be able to expect a bit of protection from God?

In the New Testament passage above, they asked Jesus 'What about those Galileans whose blood Pilate mingled with their sacrifices?' But he did not answer, because there is no satisfactory answer. Instead, he dealt with the real problem behind the question and said, 'Unless you repent, you will all likewise perish.' Jesus urged them to change the direction of their lives (for that is what repentance means) and start to look at things from God's perspective, not just their own.

So what about us? How might a change of perspective be for us? When a friend is ill, I pray for them because prayer is not just a list of requests. It is a revolutionary step in allowing God to reshape my thoughts to be more like his thoughts. Jesus taught his followers to pray: 'May Your kingdom come.'

The Kingdom of God is not a place or system. It simply describes what life is like when things are done God's way, not ours. Do I still pray with hope for healing or protection? Yes. He has created the human body, which often has miraculous and astounding powers of recovery. When we stop expecting God to jump through our hoops and think like us, then we welcome him to transform our thinking. We know from the Bible that his way may include healing and protection but that God is not a slot machine. He is not tamed by us, to do just what we demand.

I love the story of Job, which is found in the Old Testament. It is a very ancient tale of a prosperous man who lives a good and upright life. God is challenged to bring misfortune (loss of property, death of close family and personal sickness and depression) to test whether Job retains his faith. He has several 'friends' who come to counsel him. In the story of Job he is offered no satisfactory answers to his cries for explanation in the face of disaster and loss. Instead, under sore provocation, we hear him say 'Even if he killed me, I'd keep on hoping.' (Job 13:15). And yes, there is exaggeration for effect in that, for I don't believe that God has a big button marked 'Smite' that sends evil down on us. But do you get the sense? Our role is to trust in spite of both the circumstances that meet our senses and the human desire for a swift and easy explanation.

So why not let go of 'our' image of how God should behave? If we persist in trying to reconcile the love of God with the problem of pain we will either go mad, lose all faith or, what to me is even worse, stubbornly cling to a set of religious platitudes that an intelligent child of 10 could see through. I do not know. Neither do you. Nor anyone else. What I do know is that Bruno trusted God regardless and would encourage me to carry on doing so in spite of everything that has happened.

Where was God on 9/11 or 7/7? Where is God in Ukraine? He is there. Weeping at the hurt done to people. Weeping, too, at the way in which people he loved and created have been so corrupted as to think that they could please him by murdering others. And he is present in the many ways in which love and tenderness and grace are shown by people – often at great risk to themselves – who comfort the dying and the injured.

No red boxer shorts. No x-ray vision. No leaping over buildings, though, to be sure, I have experienced countless acts of loving grace in my life.

Instead God loved us so much that he came here himself, Jesus, to be wounded and die as such a powerful demonstration of selfless love that we might be released from our old ways and tired thinking about life. To be invited to turn around the direction of our lives. And so that, whatever life may throw at us, we have the promise of God with us.

* * ♦ * *

TUESDAY LUNCHTIME

Three high, grey buildings towered over the east of the town centre, each with a long ramp of concrete rising from a dismal courtyard. Some of the windows had colourful flags that brightened up the dull facades. It was a spring day, but the warmth and light had fled the towering structures. This was Southend, it would seem, twinned with Mordor.

He started to walk up the concrete ramp and noticed two men in puffer jackets loitering by the entrance, smoking hand-rolled cigarettes. Their eyes traced his progress up the ramp, leaving him feeling uneasy but determined not to let it show. He had to turn his back to use the intercom and he knew they were looking and listening as he pressed the button for the flat he had been invited to. Then the front door buzzer sounded and he slipped quickly inside, closing it behind him. He walked directly to the flat. Holding the door open, a woman gave a greeting and invited him inside. He followed her down the hallway, noticing that she had a pronounced limp. Why, he wondered – too shy to ask. On either side were doors leading into empty rooms.

Then the hall opened into a living room where an older, smiling woman sat in a comfy chair. On the far side of the room another door led, he guessed, to the kitchen. From that direction came a savoury smell of baked potatoes, along with a cluster of voices engaged in bringing together the ingredients of lunch.

"Make yourself at home" he was told, so he chose a place at the far end of a sofa and made himself comfortable. A glance around the room offered familiar sights: postcards and knick-knacks and a large TV. A mug of builder's hot tea was set down next to him on a coaster: milk, no sugar and 'as it comes'. The elderly lady in the cosy chair beamed at him and asked how he was. It was plain that those who were gathering had been told to expect a visitor but nobody knew more than that, including a name. That little group were used to having occasional visitors, as well as inviting strangers met on the street back to share their lunchtime meals.

A bright, smiling woman emerged from the kitchen, said 'Hello!' and welcomed him again. Then turning to glance back on to the kitchen worktop, she said: "I'm not sure we're going to have enough food. Where are my car keys? Give me 10 minutes and I'll be back." And with that she was gone. When she returned, she was accompanied by the two men from the front ramp of the flats of whom the visitor had been so wary on the way in. It is so easy to make judgments by appearances alone. These two guys were members of that little community. In the woman's arms was a container full of hot, freshly-fried chicken from a local shop; the fragrance quickly filled the room. As if on cue, at that point a further two friends arrived and, without any further fuss, they sat on the sofa, another armchair and on the carpet just where they could, to share that meal of fried chicken, baked potato and salad.

Everyone was friendly, blending eating with politely including their visitor in their conversation. They were curious about him, of course, but they didn't pry too much or ask detailed questions. Each one knew that too many questions might not be welcome. After plates had been emptied and collected, there was a pudding with warm custard. It seemed expected, as though a meal without a dessert was somehow a missed opportunity. Then more tea.

It was a spring day, soon after Easter, so once the meal was over, they settled back against the cushions, each holding their mug, to watch a video chosen by a member of the group. It was a dramatic reconstruction of the crucifixion of Jesus, designed to be as searingly realistic as possible. Looking around, the visitor could see that everyone in the room watched the screen intently and with tears in their eyes.

He had to wipe his own eyes too. It came home to him at that moment, as he sat with a group of friendly strangers, having been made at home and eaten with them, that it was a long, long time since he had shed tears over the events about which those in ordained ministry spoke often, and perhaps too glibly.

* * ♦ * *

That same day two of them were walking to the village Emmaus, about seven miles out of Jerusalem. They were deep in conversation, going over all these things that had happened. In the middle of their talk and questions, Jesus came up and walked along with them. But they were not able to recognize who he was. He asked, "What's this you're discussing so intently as you walk along?" They just stood there, long-faced, like they had lost their best friend. Then one of them, his name was Cleopas, said, "Are you the only one in Jerusalem who hasn't heard what's happened during the last few days?" He said, "What has happened?"

They said, "The things that happened to Jesus the Nazarene. He was a man of God, a prophet, dynamic in work and word, blessed by both God and all the people. Then our high priests and leaders betrayed him, got him sentenced to death, and crucified him. And we had our hopes up that he was the One, the One about to deliver Israel. And it is now the third day since it happened. But now some of our women have completely confused us. Early this morning they were at the tomb and couldn't find his body. They came back with the story that they had seen a vision of angels who said he was alive. Some of our friends went off to the tomb to check and found it empty just as the women said, but they didn't see Jesus."

Then he said to them, "So thick-headed! So slow-hearted! Why can't you simply believe all that the prophets said? Don't you see that these things had to happen, that the Messiah had to suffer and only then enter into his glory?" Then he started at the beginning, with the Books of Moses, and went on through all the Prophets, pointing out everything in the Scriptures that referred to him. They came to the edge of the village where they were headed. He acted as if he were going on but they pressed him: "Stay and have supper with us. It's nearly evening; the day is done." So he went in with them. And here is what happened: He sat down at the table with them. Taking the bread, he blessed and broke and gave it to them. At that moment, open-eyed, wide-eyed, they recognized him. And then he disappeared.

Back and forth they talked. "Didn't we feel on fire as he conversed with us on the road, as he opened up the Scriptures for us?" They didn't waste a minute. They were up and on their way back to Jerusalem. They found the Eleven and their friends gathered together, talking away: "It's really happened! The Master has been raised up—Simon saw him!" Then the two went over everything that happened on the road and how they recognized him when he broke the bread.

While they were saying all this, Jesus appeared to them and said, "Peace be with you." Luke 24: 13-35

Here they are, companions on the road, having left the rest of the Master's friends to walk back to their home in Emmaus. It's about seven miles away from Jerusalem. Then Jesus himself joins them, although they are kept from recognising him. He asks them very directly what they are talking about as they walk along.

Now I do not think this could easily happen where I live. I don't think a stranger could walk up to two people engrossed in conversation, walk alongside them and then ask them so directly what they are talking about.

Try it sometime on the Fenchurch Street line or in the supermarket queue but don't blame me if people look at you oddly or you get thumped.

Yet in the culture of first century Judea, they responded openly to his question, sharing their confusion and hurt. They told him about the women, about the empty tomb and about what had happened. Jesus responds equally directly and rebukes them. He calls them 'thick-headed'. Then he goes on to explain all that the prophets had foretold about him.

Imagine Jesus, walking with Cleopas and his friend, at a human pace of 3 miles per hour. I often live my life much faster than that. I hurry. I rush from one place to another. But Jesus, who walks with them at their speed, patiently explains what they might have seen more clearly if they had slowed down, listened and really looked. God doesn't hurry. I believe he walks with us, at our pace. I think that we often miss God who is right there beside us, because we are in such a hurry.

This is the moment when the story reveals its surprise. Jesus acts as if he wants to continue. He will not force himself on them, but they offer him their hospitality, as is the custom in the Middle East. They would not let him go on when night is falling. So they ask him to stay with them for food, for shelter and for friendship - those basic human needs.

They don't make a big deal out of this - no English-style fussing about telling Jesus to 'excuse the mess' or that they don't have a fancy meal to offer him. They just invite him in to share what they have. Hospitality helps friendships to grow. Food, shelter and companionship are all connected. In such ways, strangers can become friends and there is room to listen and to understand better.

And then see what happens! Our two sad and tired disciples, who have walked with Jesus, now recognize him. It is not when they are busy in their argument, absorbed by their own thoughts and understanding but at this peaceful moment, where they pause to give thanks for their daily bread and stop to eat.

As a wise scholar once remarked, *"It was at an ordinary meal in an ordinary house, when an ordinary loaf was being divided, that these men recognized Jesus."* [ii] It was in that very everyday act of slowing down to eat a meal together that they suddenly recognized Jesus. It was in the ordinary that they saw him and recognised him for who he was. It is in the ordinary tasks of everyday and when we slow down that we may get to hear him.

Then their eyes were opened. Then they received the gift of seeing Jesus for who he really is, not who they had imagined. This is a gift of the Holy Spirit. Our senses need to be awakened to recognize Christ, just as they were for those first disciples - at the table, in the garden, on the lake and on the beach. On the road to Damascus and maybe on the road to London too.

Jesus disappears from their sight and, right away,

they get up. Leaving their meal on the table, they go back the seven miles to Jerusalem. They are so moved by their experience that they risk travelling at night in order to hurry back to the city. There they find the disciples and others gathered, hearing that Jesus had risen as the women had said, and had been seen by Simon Peter. And so Cleopas and his friend share their news of what had happened 'on the way', on their journey with the three-mile-an-hour-God, and how they recognized him at the table.

When leaders make room for others to share how Christ has spoken to them, those are some of the most striking moments when Jesus is heard among a group of believers. Our faith may grow when we welcome others' glimpses of Jesus, though they may be different to our own.

We never hear of Cleopas again after this passage, and we never learn the name of his companion. Our curiosity about them is not important. They are 'ordinary' people, just like us, who have the unsettling adventure of following Jesus and meeting him in unexpected ways and finding their lives are upturned by that.

Isn't this close to our experience? We catch a glimpse of Jesus here and there; now and then. He's not often easily seen or heard. The words of the poet Gerard Manley Hopkins fit my experience: *'I greet him the days I meet him, and bless when I understand.'* [iii]

This account is remarkable because it happens in an ordinary situation. I can understand why Jesus would show himself to his 11 disciples, to the loyal women who followed him, and even to the fire-beathing Saul: all very useful appearances for establishing the church and its mission. But Cleopas and his friend are nobodies from Nowheresville: unknown people from a small village who have no clue what God is doing. They could be any of us. Their road to Emmaus is a normal road, the road each of us travels every day. This is what makes this story different from the other stories of Jesus' Easter appearances.

This tale tells us about the God who walks with human confusion, human pain and our poor faith and hope. It speaks to me where I am. Maybe most importantly, Emmaus reminds us that it is God who seeks us out.

It is not always by mustering a strong faith and a deep spirituality that we connect with the risen Christ. We can meet him in simple gestures of hospitality and friendship. Jesus walks with us at our pace. He is there, right next to us, though we often don't notice him and find it hard to see him. We may hear his voice or see what he is doing when we hush our constant talk and stream of ideas and when we make time to listen to him through the scriptures and through the voices of others. In this gospel story, we see this happening in meals, journeys, among friends and in the ordinary activities of life. So today, will you and I dare to silence the noise and slow down the pace, to listen and maybe understand a little more?

"Lord Jesus, stay with us. Be our companion in the way, kindle our hearts and awaken hope, that we may know you as you are revealed in scripture and the breaking of bread. Grant this for the sake of your love. Through Jesus Christ our Lord. Amen "[iv]

* * ♦ * *

JOHN RICHARDSON

On the 10th of January 1841 a two-masted, square rigged cargo ship known as the *William Thompson* of Sunderland put into the West India dock in London's east end to unload her cargo.

A wooden ship of 200 tons unladen weight, she carried cargo along the East Coast of England, as well as crossing the North Sea to ports in France, the Netherlands and Scandinavia. Her skipper was John Richardson, newly married and at 26 considered young to hold a master's ticket. He had been born to the sea. Born in Lisbon, on board another British sailing vessel of which his father was master. The sea was his home.

So what was it like on board the *William Thompson*? She was what was called a 'snow', from a corruption of the Dutch *snau* meaning beak, owing to the very sharply blunt pointed prow of the ship. A bewildering range of ropes and sails; wooden decks with the space between the boards filled with oakum. The rich smell of tar and stench of bilge. The deafening noise arising from the industry aboard hundreds of vessels, large and small. The crew comprised the mate, John Thackery and five hands including some apprentices. The crew depended upon one another for each safe voyage and looked to the master and mate for their greater experience in seamanship.

In the 1840s, the West India dock was a very busy place and that January day the *William Thompson* moored alongside other vessels, jostling for position. Once the cargo had been unloaded, the master went below decks to his cabin to check the strongbox kept on the shelf. The box held the 16 gold sovereigns and 6 half-sovereigns which served as his working funds for ship's maintenance and operations. He locked the strongbox and put it back on the shelf and, leaving the room, securely locked the cabin door. Telling the mate, Thackery, that he was going ashore, he stepped off the ship, left the dock and headed out westward to attend to business matters in London three miles away.

At 2pm, Thackery the mate also went ashore to have a drink in one of the local pubs and to find something to eat. Then, leaving just two of the apprentice lads on board, the others also left to explore what the largest city in the world at that time had to offer some young men with time and money on their hands.

At 4 o'clock, the mate returned and shortly after the skipper also came back on board. Going below decks, the skipper found his cabin door had been forced. The strongbox now lay on his bunk. The lock had been jemmied open: the 16 gold sovereigns and 6 half-sovereigns were gone!

Immediately, he summoned Jim Coleridge, one of the ship's apprentices who had remained on board throughout the afternoon and asked who had been seen below decks in his absence. It seemed that apprentice John Seabright had taken some of his dockside mates, Smith and Neelin, onboard and they had been seen to leave the vessel in great haste afterwards, heading off (they said) to the Surrey Theatre music hall at the southern end of London Bridge. The master left the ship without delay and set off in pursuit, collecting police constable William Sladden (number K50) from Stepney Police Station. Together they made their way to the Surrey Theatre in time to arrest Seabright as he left the stalls of the music hall, his dockside friends having disappeared. The only money he had on his person was half a sovereign, thirteen shillings and one penny. He could not explain where any of the remaining money could be found and denied having stolen it. He claimed not to have seen either of his two friends for some time. The master committed him into the charge of the constable.

The case against John Seabright came up at London's central criminal court, the infamous Old Bailey, on 1 February 1841, which meant that the *William Thompson* and her crew had to lay over, losing revenue from their cargo so that her crew might serve as witnesses. Seabright disputed the evidence of the crew but was found guilty and given, for then, the remarkably lenient sentence of 6 months in prison. Since the defendant ahead of him, a 13 year-old boy, had been given a sentence of both prison and a whipping, he was lucky. Smith and Neelin were never caught or charged.

The *William Thompson* soon acquired a new cargo and left London to resume her voyages to the continent. She foundered in a North Sea gale some years later under a different master.

So why this story? How can it have impacted me, born 120 years later? Well, there is just one additional detail that I have omitted. John Richardson and his wife, Mary Ann, had a son, also called John. One of his sons had 5 children, of whom the youngest, in turn. had a daughter and…me. The ship's master's full name was John Richardson King. He was my great-great-grandfather.

* * ♦ * *

The sons of Noah who came out of the ark were Shem, Ham and Japheth. (Ham was the father of Canaan.) These were the three sons of Noah, and from them came the people who were scattered over the whole earth. Genesis 9:18

Like so many others, I have been captured by the fascinating world of genealogy: that is, family history. My mother started to research our family tree in the 1970s before it really became so fashionable. I can remember that her findings were recorded on a long roll of lining paper and that itself was quite fun because as the paper unrolled you saw different branches of your family appear before you. My sister has researched our family roots in a much more systematic and rigorous way and so we now know the names and, sometimes the occupations, of people from several generations ago. It was after my sister had her DNA analysed that we discovered, on one side of the family, an apparent anomaly, suggesting an unexpected and quite prominent Scottish ancestry, when our direct knowledge and all the evidence suggested none. It turns out that one of our parents had a strong Celtic genetic component, whereas the other side of the family were from the much more expected East Anglia.

On my mother's side there were generations of farm workers living in Norfolk. On Dad's side, I find the story above fascinating. It opens a window into the life and experience of someone who my paternal grandfather might have known as 'granddad'. His life experience was very different to my own, not simply because we live in different times but because of John Richardson King's own roots which almost certainly steered the direction of his life. He was born in Lisbon to British parents (quite possibly onboard ship). His father, John Whittingham King, was another ship's master, so it looks as though he was born to the sea. Beyond this glimpse into his working life as well as his wife Mary Ann's name and the number of children that they had together, we know no more about JRK. We do know that his son John Emmanuel King was not a seaman. He came south from the north-east and became a court clerk, which is somewhat closer to my work experience. Sadly, he hit hard times: some of his children, including my grandfather and at least some of his siblings spent time as children in the workhouse. The fascination of genealogy is not simply in discovering facts about ancestors but, where possible, something of the fabric and detail of their lives.

What is it about this sense of being rooted among a group of names about whom we know so little? What is it that gives us our sense of belonging in family and our home in fixed places?

I discovered in a recent article that all people with blue eyes, as I have, can trace a common ancestor who came out of Africa and migrated through what is now Turkey a defined number of generations ago. The theory of degrees of separation, which purports to show the connectedness of all human beings in one way or another, is supported by all blue-eyed people sharing a common ancestor.

I am an amateur storyteller. I usually tell European folk tales but I also love to tell some of the Old Testament stories. All of them are truthful; some have greater historicity. Did the serpent really speak aloud to Eve? I am not really concerned to know if there was a literal Eve or if the serpent was audibly loquacious. I am much more interested in what the serpent said.[v] What I like to say to congregations when I am telling Bible stories is that these are our stories too. Or, more accurately, we are part of the same continuing account of faith that included Abraham, Isaac and Jacob. The episodes of the story that included Moses, Ruth, Esther and Elijah all took place in our continuing story, just a long way ahead of us. Those who went before us, thousands of years ago or much more recently, played their part in moulding the people that we are now.

I am also fascinated by the extent to which faith and belief can be traced back across the generations. I don't just mean that church attendance and being part of a Sunday School were more commonplace in previous generations, leading to people being more familiar with Bible stories than they are today. Looking back over the family tree I can see at least two people of faith, aside from those I knew personally. One had the forenames Theodore Theophilus (gift of God and friend of God), so I suspect his parents probably stitched up his future at birth. Alongside this, one great-grandfather was given a commendation by his church for opening his house as a meeting place, with a window kept open early each morning to hand out food to hungry street kids on their way to school. The same man was expelled by another nonconformist congregation for having an occasional smoke and drink! The triumph of religion over an active faith, I feel. That church lost a good man.

Who knows how our ancestors saw or thought of God? I do not know what part God played in the life of John Richardson King. I suspect that there will have been times when his wooden-hulled sailing vessel was in a North Sea gale or nearing the treacherous sandbanks of the Humber or Thames Estuaries when, maybe, a prayer might have crossed his lips.

Thank you, God, for those in our families who have lived their lives before we were born. Even when we don't know their names, you knew them and loved them, just as much as you know and love us.

* * ♦ * *

DAVID

<u>A letter to the Coroner – October 2005</u>

By now, Madam, you will have been notified of the unexplained death of David K. I write on behalf of this church to which David belonged, to share our concern that the cause of his death needs to be established. As members of his community of friends, we respectfully suggest that questions should be asked about the care (or lack of it) that may have contributed to his premature death.

I knew David K and his father for 18 months. Firstly, they were members of the congregation I serve as a minister. Yet they were also close neighbours, living for most of this period opposite my family home. I saw David and his father each Sunday morning at church, where they were regular attenders, and more frequently (sometimes daily) as visitors to my home. They were citizens of Iran who had come to the UK to seek treatment for David's chronic poor health. Yet there was another reason for their living away from home: though his father remained a Muslim, David had converted to Christianity. Iran is not a safe place for converts from Islam.

David had severe epilepsy, with several fits each

day. He took a bewildering number of prescribed drugs to mitigate his condition. These were administered lovingly by his father, not least when David was in the throes of a seizure. David was also a very heavy smoker of rough tobacco. At no time during the past 18-months was his health robust. Father and son lived on very little money and David seemed to subsist on bottled water, eggs and tobacco. He barely slept and, on occasions when I was awake in the night, I could see him seated in the oriel bay window of their first floor flat in the depths of night, staring out.

During 2005 there was a noticeable decline in his physical and mental wellbeing. Physically, his father estimates that he lost around 20kgs of body weight in the last 6 months or so. While I am unable to be precise about this figure, a loss of that scale would fit my own observations. He began to lose balance while standing and found walking more difficult as, eventually, his legs could not bear even that reduced weight easily. When I last saw him on 6 October, he could not stand at all and required a wheelchair. He could not hold his head erect. He was gaunt and desperately thin. Later that day, his father visited my home to ask for help since David was once again on the floor and could not summon the strength to stand.

In terms of his mental health, increasingly he spoke of events as fact that plainly could not have been true. His first language was Farsi. His English, though poor, was adequate for basic communication when I first met him. Throughout this year, however, he became far less coherent and would link disparate ideas in sentences believing that they had significance; in reality, they were nonsense.

It seemed both to me, and to a highly experienced social worker in membership of our church, that David was malnourished and we believed he might be a victim of unintentional neglect. We became so concerned about his wellbeing that I wrote to the Chief Community Care Officer of the local authority, seeking urgent assessments of his mental and physical states. I was telephoned subsequently by a council social worker, to inform me that he was already working with the K family. He was unaware of the problems around weight loss and mental confusion. At my urgent request, an Approved Social Worker was called in and I was present at an assessment which took place, at the church. It was confirmed by the ASW that there was sufficient evidence to merit an evaluation by a psychiatrist. David and his father were asked if they would be willing to go to a hospital for this and they agreed.

Although I saw Mr K senior several times in the days following, that was the last occasion I saw David. Just over a week later, the family was obliged to move to another flat around a mile away. On the day of the move, the neighbour living in the flat below them saw David as he left the house in a wheelchair, his head lolling. He described David's complexion as 'mustard coloured'.

I understand that David died in the early hours of

Monday, 17 October 2005. I picked up a voicemail from his father who was terribly distressed. At his urgent request I went round to find the new flat. Quite understandably this was being treated as a potential crime scene. David was still a young man; his death was unexplained and his body was surrounded by countless tablets and capsules which had spilled over the bedding and all over the floor. His father was arrested on suspicion of involvement in the death of his son and taken to Ilford police station. I followed on and persuaded the investigating officer that Mr K was highly vulnerable and that I could serve as an appropriate adult to accompany him through his interviews. David's father was greatly distressed that his son's body would be subject to an autopsy and retained pending an inquest. In Islam, the presumption is for the earliest possible burial. Released on bail, David's father returned to Iran after petitioning the local mosques to pay for his son's funeral.

Over the last 18 months, David was visited by paramedics and taken to King George Hospital Accident and Emergency Department on several occasions. Sometimes I telephoned for the ambulance; on other occasions I visited David in the treatment area of A&E or collected him when he was assessed fit for discharge. Although there were communication problems and the family was reticent or embarrassed about their circumstances, he seemed to me to be self-evidently malnourished and confused. Allowing for this, was it right that he was discharged (or allowed to discharge himself) without questions being asked about his general mental and physical wellbeing?

On at least one occasion, he claimed that he was assaulted by security staff of the hospital. Given his mental confusion, I think this is unlikely to be true though they may perhaps have needed to restrain him. He did seem to become more aggressive at times in the last few months.

During the time I knew him, David was also a patient of two successive General Practitioners in Ilford and also at the Royal London Hospital. Was it not apparent to any of these professionals that he was dangerously underweight?

I have no reason to believe that David's father, who was his sole carer, offered him anything but loving care, at some considerable cost to himself. Accompanying his son meant that the father had had to leave his wife and other children in Iran. However, given that his father's English was very poor, together with the complexity of the range of powerful drugs that David was prescribed, I am concerned that his father may not have been competent to administer them safely. I made this point in my letter to the local authority and also face to face when I saw the family's social worker in October.

I do not raise these concerns lightly. It may be that no earlier intervention would have prevented David's death. The church does not seek to apportion blame now. Yet we, his friends, respectfully suggest that these issues need to be explored to establish if there are lessons for the statutory agencies to learn. I would be willing to present evidence and be questioned in the inquest, if that is the course of action you feel to be right.

Yours,

———————————

Not long afterwards, the Coroner's officer notified all the interested parties that there would be an inquest. He said that the coroner would like me to give evidence along the lines of the points made in my letter. On the day of the inquest I attended the Coroner's Court, dressed formally but without anything to indicate that I was a Christian minister. As we queued outside the court, I heard one of the expert witnesses – police? medic? pathologist? I cannot now remember – ask aloud why they were all there wasting time on such a pointless exercise? Another witness spoke up in reply: 'Because some ****** fool of a priest has gone and stuck his oar in.'

As the inquest went on the coroner noted that, aside from his father, the church had been the only consistently supportive network for David. In the absence of his father, she welcomed the church to stand-in informally in place of his family and ask the expert witnesses any questions.

She agreed from the post-mortem photographs that David's body had the appearance of a concentration camp victim. None of the doctors who gave evidence would comment upon why they had discharged him, often several times, in that condition. At the conclusion of the inquest, the coroner recorded a narrative verdict. David had died following a massive grand-mal attack; just one more after the many hundreds he had suffered in the course of his life. While she sympathised with the concerns of the church community, she did not feel able to make any mention of David's care and treatment as a contributory factor to his death.

* * ♦ * *

Suppose one of you had a hundred sheep and lost one. Wouldn't you leave the ninety-nine in the wilderness and go after the lost one until you found it? When found, you can be sure you would put it across your shoulders, rejoicing, and when you got home call in your friends and neighbours, saying, 'Celebrate with me! I've found my lost sheep!' Count on it—there's more joy in heaven over one sinner's rescued life than over ninety-nine good people in no need of rescue. Luke 15: 4-7

Jesus told parables to get people thinking more about what God is like by shaking them out of simply repeating the moralising religion that required no thought, simply compliance. The parables that Jesus tells are all intended to create a reaction. The reaction might be puzzlement - people just scratched their heads because they didn't know the answer. It might be laughter or tears or possibly provoking listeners to such anger that they wanted to hit someone – sometimes Jesus himself. You see the parables are not simple moral tales told by a teacher who wags his finger and says 'do this' or 'don't do that'. They are much more powerful than that.

It is when we are confronted with uncomfortable situations that we begin to discover whether or not our faith is mere religion or has some life-giving substance and power to it. For if God is at work in us, slowly re-coding our spiritual DNA to take the character of Jesus, then we will find ourselves again and again in situations which push our faith to the limits. Sometimes that will be among uncomfortable people and in tight corners.

The story that Jesus tells about the lost sheep is one that would have made the first hearers laugh out loud. What sheer stupidity! Leaving ninety-nine healthy sheep unattended to go looking for one sheep. To lose one sheep might be an acceptable loss but to endanger ninety-nine through neglect would be madness. In the story set out above in the letter to the coroner, it would be tempting to depict David as someone with whom it made little sense to spend much time. He is chronically sick; incurably so. He and his father are foreigners, easily dismissed by professionals as health refugees. They do not speak English well and their culture and language is as strange to us as ours is to them. But, while we may choose to look away, they have nowhere else to turn.

Similar people are found in several stories in the Bible. We are reminded that the evidence of our faith is not simply in worship or ritual but in how we relate to other people and, in particular, those who are the most vulnerable. In the very first book of the Bible we find the story of Cain and Abel. It's only 4 chapters in from the beginning if you would like to read it for yourself. Cain acts out of jealousy and kills his brother. When God asks Cain where his brother might be, Cain famously shouts: "Am I my brother's keeper?", to which the silent but well-understood response is 'Yes'. We are indeed our brothers' (and sisters') keepers. Jesus had this to say:

Then the King will say to those on his right, 'Enter, you who are blessed by my Father! Take what's coming to you in this kingdom. It's been ready for you since the world's foundation. And here's why:

I was hungry and you fed me,
I was thirsty and you gave me a drink,
I was homeless and you gave me a room,
I was shivering and you gave me clothes,
I was sick and you stopped to visit,
I was in prison and you came to me.'

"Then those 'sheep' are going to say, 'Master, what are you talking about? When did we ever see you hungry and feed you, thirsty and give you a drink? And when did we ever see you sick or in prison and come to you?' Then the King will say, 'I'm telling the solemn truth: Whenever you did one of these things to someone overlooked or ignored, that was me—you did it to me.' Matthew 25: 34-40

Some Christians carry in their minds an image of the triumphant Christ. Yet the gospel writers also show us, at points, the vulnerable Christ. The one who had led and taught and challenged and acted became the one who was led, listened in silence, was flogged and executed. In the resurrection encounters, he continues to bear the scars of his suffering. There are some more reflections on his vulnerability towards the end of this book.

I do not find it hard to see Christ in the slumped, jaundiced, wheelchair-bound figure of David. Nor to believe that, in challenging the casual case-management of the many professionals whose 'care' he received, that we were seeking some recognition; some justice for this man – our friend. He was someone who had no standing, literally or figuratively. In seeking answers and some accountability, it was David and Christ for whom we spoke up.

We see beauty in stained glass and sunsets and marvel at the artistry of the divine. Such things may draw our eyes away from the Christ who lolls, jaundiced, in the wheelchair at our elbow.

* * ♦ * *

Part Two

YOUR OWN STORY

* * ♦ * *

HELEN

In a group of welcoming strangers in someone's sitting room, it was your hoot of laughter that marked you out as somebody who enjoyed a joke and would be worth getting to know.

It was all new to us. Newlyweds, and in a part of London which was unknown to us both. We were freshly arrived at the church at the end of the road. We had decided that we would start with the nearest one and see what that was like. If that didn't work out, then we would enlarge our search in a spiral from our first-floor bedsit, until we found somewhere where we felt comfortable and could join in.

We turned up at our first service at 6.30 that winter's evening, because by tradition every Baptist Church had an evening service at that time. Except this one. They had moved the evening service to 5pm during the winter months, better to suit older people who didn't want to be out late and in the cold. They took pity on us, invited us to return the following Sunday morning. The lady with the amazing smile rushed to hand over a bouquet of flowers from the display in the church as a welcome present.

When we started to settle-in we paid a visit to the nearest midweek group, which is where we met you, Helen. Friendly, Scottish, larger than life and with that hoot of laughter.

On each of those evenings, tea would be taken into the sitting room. The children of the house would politely say goodnight and then we would settle down to catch-up, listen to and discuss some words usually from the New Testament before saying our prayers together. Maybe 8 or so people each week. You would take part in the group while also knitting intricate patterns, at which you were amazingly skilled.

Our first home was a bedsit in a house we shared with seven other people and one tank of hot water. The young builder who left the house at 6am daily kindly emptied the hot water tank with his bath. So it was a very welcome move a few months later from there to our first flat on the ground floor of a house in Seven Kings, the next station up the line. Now with a kitchen of our own, you were one of the first people who came to share food with us. I collected you one night from your flat just down the road from the church and brought you back to eat and watch television while you knitted another intricate pattern. At the end of the evening I drove you home but – and I still don't know how this happened - we must have caught a trailing thread of wool outside the doors of the Triumph Toledo. By the time we had driven the mile or so to your flat, little remained of the carefully knitted garment. Instead, there was a long trail of yarn stretching back around the streets of Ilford.

Little by little, as friendship and trust grew, you told us some of your life story. About your only brother who had drowned and your father who had been a policeman, prone at times to being heavy-handed. We had the fun of meeting your Mum, a delightful lady of faith, who sometimes came to visit from Scotland.

After we had known you for quite a while, you asked if you might make me a present of a jumper. Having seen the superb quality of your knitting, I asked for a cream Aran cable-knit jumper and, having bought the wool, you set to making this with a skill that was stunning. I was called to a fitting to check that it was a good length and looked forward very much to receiving my new, soft and warm winter jumper.

No one quite knows what happened. For when the jumper was ready it was perfect in every respect, with intricate patterning and a robust rib to cuffs and hem. It was also (and I smile now as I write this) about 60 centimetres in length too long. Home knitted garments tend to have less tension than machine knitted ones but this reached down to my knees!

A good friend and very able craftswoman from church kindly unpicked 30 centimetres of the jumper before reattaching the ribbing. It was still too long. So my mother repeated the exercise and a further 30 centimetres was removed. From that point on, as long as I wore a belt above the jumper and concealed this with a fold of the pattern, I had the most beautiful, soft and warm top for the coldest of seasons.

Life was often not easy for you, Helen. You had known loss and unhappiness, although you had found love and acceptance among a church community of what were strangers to begin with in Ilford, a long way from Glasgow. You sometimes found life difficult to cope with and were understandably frustrated and angry when things did not go well. You also had an amazing gift of insight. There were times when, within the church family, we were unable to agree about the way forward. There were meetings I attended and which finished after midnight. Yet, first thing the next morning, you would contact me to ask about something that no one had told you about but which had occurred when most others were already in bed the night before. That happened more than once.

Then, one day, you had a stroke. I came to visit you in King George Hospital. I entered the ward wondering how badly the stroke might have affected you, physically or mentally. As you saw me standing at your bedside, I realised then that you recognised somebody whom you knew and loved but it wasn't me. Thinking I was Jesus, you asked me why it was that I had given you this stroke.

There are moments in life and in loving one's friends and strangers when it really helps to be nimble in your thinking and reaction. To have argued, explained and insisted who I really was would not have helped but would have caused greater frustration and confusion. So, with trepidation and a sudden silent prayer, I replied as someone representing Christ. I told you that I had not sent the debilitating stroke but that some things just happen. I told you that I loved you and that I would always be with you.

It has been my hesitant privilege to represent Christ and his church in a number of ways since, though never quite so directly. Yet, as I write these words, I have an assurance that what was said and the spirit in which it was spoken was something that helped you, Helen, and was also true and right for that moment.

The other shared memory that I now commit to words was of a single room in that same hospital, in the sweltering heat of a summer gone mad. I took my turn in the rota of friends from church who – also representing the presence of Christ - sat quietly by your bedside, praying silent prayers and keeping you company in your final hours. It fell to me to be with you when you died. Your death was imperceptible and peaceful. It took me a few moments to realise you were no longer breathing.

You faced many trials in this life. You had what, nowadays, we would call a learning disability. Aspects of your appearance made you prone to bullying. You knew tragedy in your family and for most of your life you lived far away from your birthplace and home culture. In later years, you suffered from depression and lost the will to take best care of yourself. Sometimes it seemed that you ploughed through friends rather quickly.

Even if that is all true, you were a fighter and a survivor. That survival was a powerful, sometimes explosive, combination of deep generosity and caring that was protected by the ability to challenge others. You would as likely cuss us out as anything else, but those close to you knew that the temper was only part of the picture. A hard life sometimes produces a hard shell around a very fragile but generous soul.

The most important thing was your faith. It would have been easy, understandable even, if you had turned your back on God years ago. But you didn't. You may not always have agreed with his timing as you perceived it. But you were friends with God in a way that was quite startling. You would talk about him as if he was there and intimately involved in whatever the topic of conversation was at the time. 'What do you think You're playing at Lord?' you would ask. Even though you argued with God (and there's a good biblical basis for that) you trusted him for comfort, for healing, for rescue, for forgiveness, for strength and in everyday life.

What do I recall now of our friendship? We made and cooked Scotch eggs together when we came to eat at your flat. Also the time you reached out to hold my hand, to quieten my nerves in a tense meeting. Your friendship, freely offered and received by someone quite different. A deep faith. And that hoot of laughter!

Helen: may you rest in peace and rise in glory.

Why have you given me this?
You asked, gazing and wondering.
The long, blue siren journey strengthening
Kilbride tones.
But, I hastened to insist,
In your pain you have invested
Me with cruel, Almighty powers.
Fearful of towering presumption
I started to protest when
Right then I knew
You did not want me to cavil or deny.
So, for one long moment,
I stood Proxy and held your hand
In divine bafflement. [vi]

* * ♦ * *

    I have never met anyone else quite like Helen. Yet she reminds me of someone with an equally distinctive character who loved God and talked with him in a natural, conversational way that many of her contemporaries found unsettling.

Margery Kempe was a woman from mediaeval England whose faith and encounters with God led her to travel the known world, meet and dispute with archbishops and other church leaders and share her faith with both proud and humble people. She was the subject of much ridicule in her home-town, throughout much of England and as far away as Rome and Jerusalem.

Margery was the first person to write about her own life in English, when she wrote The Book of Margery Kempe[vii]. She was born in 1373 in King's Lynn in Norfolk, where her father was a rich merchant and the mayor. She married John Kempe and had 14 children with him. They ran a brewery business. After her first child was born, she suffered from a mental breakdown and heard voices that told her to do evil things. She bit her hand to stop herself from killing herself and the scar stayed with her until she died. She was very close to the spiritual world and felt God and Jesus speaking to her directly. Margery was not shy about sharing these spiritual experiences with others. She said that she had conversations with God and Jesus, which challenged the authority of the church and the clergy who claimed to be the only ones who could connect with God. She cried a lot because of her sins and also God's mercy, which she felt very strongly.

Margery told people that Jesus lived in her soul. But she also had doubts and questions. She sought advice from priests and religious people, some of whom were supportive and some of whom were hostile. Some thought she was sincere and honest, others thought she was a troublemaker or a heretic who deserved to be burned at the stake.

The church in England in the early 1400s was worried about the influence of a group called the 'Lollards'. They followed John Wycliffe, who was the first to translate the whole Bible into English. Wycliffe and his followers had some ideas that were similar to the Reformation that followed later. They wanted the Bible to be in English so that ordinary people could understand it and they thought that worshipping saints was like worshipping idols. Margery was not a Lollard and she tried to show that she was faithful to the Catholic church, but she was accused of being a heretic several times. One reason for this might have been that she taught from the scripture in English, which was not allowed by the church at that time.

Margery made several pilgrimages, the longest and most difficult of which was a journey to Jerusalem, with a long stopover in Rome. Margery was stranded in that city for a time after giving away her money to the poor. She was shunned by her travelling companions who were embarrassed by her piety which compared unfavourably with their greedy and bawdy behaviour. She was forced to beg in order to survive. As in so many other places, Margery's frequent and loud tears bewailing her faults begin to draw unwelcome attention to her and she became notorious, making enemies among the resident English community in Rome. Even so, Margery was accepted as a holy woman by some, and her advice and blessings were sought by those humble enough to see God at work in her. Margery later accompanied her widowed daughter-in-law when she returned to her native Germany along the Baltic coast (nowadays part of Poland). The longer of the two accounts of Margery's life ends with Margery returning to King's Lynn. There she cared for her husband, who seems to have developed dementia in his early 60s.

It was highly unusual for a woman to have such an impact on society in the Middle Ages, to be so widely travelled or to have theological conversations with the patriarchy of the church. In teaching and speaking openly about God and theology, Margery stood against the male-centred norms of her time and culture. She was a disturber of the settled pattern of life, which is why she faced such opposition and personal abuse. She was tried for heresy multiple times but never convicted. She also met some other formative figures in the mediaeval English church, such as the female anchorite Julian of Norwich, to share her visions and experiences. It seems that, though very different in temperament, Margery and Dame Julian recognised and appreciated the glimpses of the divine that they saw in one another.

It is important that we do not look at Margery's life and experiences through a 21st century lens. She was a creature of her time and her writings are set in the context of a society where religion infused every aspect of life. We now live in a very different age and culture. Yet I feel that Margery and Helen are soulmates.

What may we learn from them? Well, it is said that we are made in the image of God.

Quite what that means is less clear. I don't believe it means that God has two arms and two legs. Instead, I think we are closer to the truth if we understand that God has placed in each one of us something that distantly reflects aspects of his nature. That may be to do with our capacity to reason, or to make the distinction between what is right and wrong; or what is loving or hateful. I am strongly attracted to the idea that, because community and relationship are at the very heart of what the Bible teaches about the nature of the threefold character of God, our being social creatures is a distant echo of God's relational nature.

So I believe that God created each individual human being with the desire to be social – to be in relationships: with other humans, with all creation and with him. He imagined us out of love and in the hope of a relationship with you and me, and each of us with one another.

When we read the scriptures through that lens it makes much more sense. For example, here are three verses:

Then the man and his wife heard the sound of the LORD *God as he was walking in the garden in the cool of the day, and they hid from the* LORD *God among the trees of the garden. But the* LORD *God called to the man, "Where are you?" Genesis 3: 8-9*

GOD *spoke with Moses face-to-face, as neighbours speak to one another. Exodus 33:11*

Then GOD *called out, "Samuel, Samuel!" Samuel answered, "Yes? I'm here." 1 Samuel 3:4-5*

And we could go on quoting other such verses.

Let's just pause for a moment and reflect upon that. Though we were all created through a physical relationship between human beings, which may have been delightful and fulfilling or a long way from that, the spark of God-given life in each one of us comes with his hope and desire that we should know him. I don't know what your life is like right now, whether you face 'weary ways or golden days', but I believe very strongly that if we grasp the truth of how God gazes upon you and me with nothing but an intense focus of love, that would go a very long way to countering the lies and distortions many of us bear about who we are.

As with all relationships, to be real it needs to be mutual. For that reason, we need to be attentive to the way in which we respond to God's constant love for us. For some, that is an intellectual thing. Their 'relationship' with God is based on analysis and reason. Others, like Margery and Helen, seem to have a more natural and personal engagement with God.

Margery Kempe and my friend Helen were highly unusual people. Sadly, often misunderstood, criticised and bullied when they should be loved and treasured. If people feel uneasy in their company or with their experiences, it often seems safer to mock or be angry than to live with the awkwardness.

* * ♦ * *

DENNIS

A young couple moved into their first little house. It was a narrow so-called artisan's cottage, built for the local workers in 1900. You, Dennis, were one of the first people they encountered in the new neighbourhood. To be truthful, it was hard to miss you.

You would march smartly and purposefully along the pavement carrying a swagger stick. From time to time, you would pause to conduct face-on inspections. Calling attention to unkempt dressing or a slack uniform, no drill-sergeant was as exacting as you in your demand for perfection. Every privet hedge was scrutinized and, having loudly reprimanded the shrub in question for its shortcomings, you would execute a swift and precise left-turn, marching off crisply in your original direction of travel.

Our young couple, like other newcomers to the district, had to make themselves stop gawping at this sight. For those who had been your neighbours for much longer, your barked orders blended-in among the birdsong and traffic noise: unremarkable in their familiarity. You would march on to whatever was that day's fixture. For you went, day by day, to whichever church was hosting a Holy Communion service that morning. Most worshippers retreated afterwards from altar to coffee servery, to a welcome cup of hot tea, a chat and some biscuits. One day it would be the United Reformed Church at Gants Hill. The next, St. George's in the Woodford Avenue, and so on.

Afterwards, having met that morning with God and his people in those different congregations, you would then resume your march in order to nurse a half-pint of bitter in the King George V – the KG5. Later that afternoon, you would stroll home. This time, with a heady mixture of low blood sugar and alcohol, your gait was an amble, lacking its earlier military drive and precision.

From time to time, young mums with pushchairs would cross the road to keep a discreet distance. Cocky youths might taunt and provoke from the other side of the street, expecting (and, oh yes, receiving!) a dusty and soldierly response, delivered in the crispest of military language.

Well, life is often improved by the occasional appearance of those who are harmlessly eccentric. In our time we have encountered dapper men most immaculately presented in lounge suits, with grey hair rendered the deepest black by the application of shoe polish. We have known a man who, having greeted the ladies of the neighbourhood politely, would discreetly reach round in order to deliver a pinch to their bottoms. Innocent that I am, I once asked directions of that young woman in the jaguar print coat and thigh length boots. It was only as I walked away with her friendly directions to my destination that I noticed the car next to her with the blacked out windows and it dawned on me that perhaps she might have been working.

So the streets of our towns are indeed full of interesting characters. Being English, of course, means that we are determined to pay no attention, no matter how gaudy the dress or egregious the behaviour. For such are always there if you simply open your eyes to see. Live and let live.

In your case though, Dennis, you soon acquired a name. You lived around the corner in the house that had belonged to your late parents many years before. Your father was long dead and your mother had slowly gone blind. It seems that she rejected the possibility of restorative surgery since that would have left you on your own to cope. And as everyone in your family, your church and the neighbourhood knew, how could Dennis possibly cope on his own?

The irony was that in the years after her death you had indeed coped but only after your own fashion. When first you allowed us into your sanctuary - a large Edwardian house which had once been well-to-do - that was the beginning of a relationship of trust that developed over the years that we lived in Westbury Road. By then much of the house was bare wood. Our first visit came about because the elements on the upturned electric fire upon which you boiled your eggs and the water for your tea had burnt out. We were able to supply a new fire which we thought (how innocently!) was to keep you warm but which quickly got upturned onto its back to serve, once again, as both fire and cooker.

In the back room in which you lived was an ancient armchair that was hopelessly filled with decades' worth of clutter. It was a fire risk as well as harbouring other unsavoury hazards. You graciously allowed a few of us to come with refuse sacks to clear some of the excess materials piled upon it and around it, subject to your scrutiny and approval of each item, taking away only what you allowed to go to the dump.

When we saw inside your house it became obvious that you had no real means of heating water to wash. It was then that the offer came to run you a hot bath once a week in our 1980s fashionably wild sage coloured bathroom and to share a hot meal afterwards. And that became a Monday evening fixture: the night Dennis would come for his bath and for dinner. You rarely said much, Dennis, beyond repeating the same question at the front door upon leaving to go home each week. Your croaky voice rendered thus by rough-cut roll up cigarettes: 'May I remain in your fellowship?'

Helping other people is not about what we can do for them. Instead it is about seeing a human being where other people only see eccentricity. A person who, locked in the safe place of their dreamworld, occasionally frightens those who don't share that understanding or see the world through your eyes.

Growing up in the 60s and 70s, there were sometimes posters bearing the hopeful and idealistic phrase 'there are no strangers, only friends we haven't yet met.' It is easy now to be cynical or dismissive of such sentiments. A me-first culture has knocked community into second place. Yet if society is a collection of minorities, we need not only to look out for one another but, where we can, to value the world 'the other' inhabits too.

Your time is now past and you no longer march down the streets of Ilford, calling the trees to attention or thrashing the hedges with your swagger stick. Your extended family (who knew?) ensured that you had a good send off at a plush Golf Club – the kind of establishment that would never have permitted you entrance in your lifetime. Still, you would have greatly enjoyed the excellent canapes.

People who were frightened of you, or who looked at you with pity or disdain, did not see the radiant child of God that you were made to be and are now. One day, Dennis, all our eyes will be opened to see you as God always did and does now.

* * ♦ * *

If you decide for God, living a life of God-worship, it follows that you don't fuss about what's on the table at mealtimes or whether the clothes in your closet are in fashion. There is far more to your life than the food you put in your stomach, more to your outer appearance than the clothes you hang on your body. Look at the birds, free and unfettered, not tied down to a job description, careless in the care of God. And you count far more to him than birds.

"Has anyone by fussing in front of the mirror ever gotten taller by so much as an inch? All this time and money wasted on fashion—do you think it makes that much difference? Instead of looking at the fashions, walk out into the fields and look at the wildflowers. They never primp or shop, but have you ever seen colour and design quite like it? The ten best-dressed men and women in the country look shabby alongside them.

"If God gives such attention to the appearance of wildflowers—most of which are never even seen—don't you think he'll attend to you, take pride in you, do his best for you? What I'm trying to do here is to get you to relax, to not be so preoccupied with getting, so you can respond to God's giving. People who don't know God and the way he works fuss over these things, but you know both God and how he works. Steep your life in God-reality, God-initiative, God-provisions. Don't worry about missing out. You'll find all your everyday human concerns will be met.

"Give your entire attention to what God is doing right now, and don't get worked up about what may or may not happen tomorrow. God will help you deal with whatever hard things come up when the time comes. Matthew 6: 25-34

Do you see the big crowd, sitting on the mountainside listening to Jesus? He isn't giving them a new set of rules to live by. Instead he describes what life is like in the kingdom of God: that is, when things are done God's way; when we live by his values and choices. He tells his listeners that they cannot serve God and money both, describing money as if it is a rival God. He then teaches that they mustn't worry or become obsessed about eating and drinking or what kind of clothes they wear. They should look at the birds which get to eat even though no one feeds them. They should see the amazing beauty of flowers as a sign of God's generous provision.

Above all, they should seek first God's Kingdom and his rightful way of behaviour and other necessities of life will be provided for them. They are not to worry about tomorrow for each day has enough stress of its own. I find it reassuring that God understands my tendency to worry.

We know from the gospel writers that many of those who came to follow Jesus were what the religious people of the day called 'sinners.' By that they meant people who, because of their poverty or circumstances of their life, were not able to observe every last tiny detail of the Law of Moses. That was the reality of life in 1st century Palestine: it was challenging for many people to find the daily necessities of life. This meant that they lacked the time and headspace to focus on religion.

Let's be clear: Jesus is not speaking here to such people but instead to those who have enough food and clothing, possessions and money and yet allow these things to be too important in life. Jesus said that it was easier for a camel to pass through the eye of a needle than for a rich person to enter the Kingdom of heaven.

We might quibble if someone said that we are rich but, if we have more than enough to eat and wear, we are richer than many; perhaps richer than most.

The cost of essential daily food has risen steeply in recent months, alongside a staggering increase in the cost of heating. In the biblical Letter of James we read this:

Dear friends, do you think you'll get anywhere in this if you learn all the right words but never do anything? Does merely talking about faith indicate that a person really has it? For instance, you come upon an old friend dressed in rags and half-starved and say, "Good morning, friend! Be clothed in Christ! Be filled with the Holy Spirit!" and walk off without providing so much as a coat or a cup of soup—where does that get you? Isn't it obvious that God-talk without God-acts is outrageous nonsense? James 2: 14-17

Those are hard-hitting words. The early church understood this. In the stories of the earliest churches that we find in the Bible's Book of Acts, chapter 11, the first Christians reacted to a severe famine over the whole Roman world. As far as they were able, each member provided help for those in other places even when they didn't know them personally or perhaps even their names.

The reflection today is for any who have enough to eat and plenty of clothes. If we truly want to have God's love at work in us, we must not obsess about this food or that food or hanker after expensive clothing – or indeed seek to have more than we need of either. Instead, whether it is a tin of beans (if that is truly what we can spare) or a multi-pack of tins or an occasional extra week's shopping for the foodbank if we can stretch to that, the reality of our faith is not just in reciting a creed or singing worship songs week by week but also in sharing what God has given us with others. Faith without action is just the stinking corpse of religion.

You see, with simple and discreet actions, we can make today better for someone else and find too that the Kingdom of God has come closer to us. On the last occasion Jesus ate with his disciples before the crucifixion, he said: *"Now that you know these things, you are blessed if you do them."*

So, having heard these things, what will you now do?

* * ◆ * *

LAURA AND ASH

My dear, dear friends, if God loved us like this, we certainly ought to love each other. No one has seen God, ever. But if we love one another, God dwells deeply within us, and his love becomes complete in us. 1 John 4:11-12.

In the name of the Father and of the Son and of the Holy Spirit. Amen.

On behalf of this church, I would like to welcome the family and friends of Ash and Laura as, with them, we celebrate this special day.

Everyone here seems to be in their place for this most wonderful occasion. Bride and groom. Minister and organist. Bridesmaids, flower girl, best man and page boy. The parents, family and friends of both bride and groom. All the guests are here. But the most important guest of all is nowhere to be seen. Where is God? For, though we meet in church today, God is nowhere to be seen.

I wonder if anyone here has ever thought of how it would be like if God was seen here among us today? What would that be like? Surely it would be the most powerful and wonderful experience we could ever have.

Listen to some of those people who have returned from the edge of death; some among them speak about a tremendously bright and beautiful light and incredible joy and peace. They are saddened at re-awakening to this life.

All of us have heard about God. Even if we do not believe there is a God, all of us have at least wondered about his existence. Those who follow Christ know his promises and we also know that here on earth we have to live by faith and not by sight. But wouldn't it be great, even for just a moment, to see God? It isn't easy to always live by faith. It would be brilliant if just once we could actually see the One in whom we believe. Yet the Bible makes clear: God cannot be seen.

'You may not see my face,' said God to Moses. 'No one can see me and live.' Exodus 33:20

However, says our text, *'if we love one another, God dwells deeply within us, and his love becomes complete in us.'*

Did you catch that? Our love for one another is evidence of God's presence right here and now, within us. If we fulfil the command to love one another, then we experience something of God's presence in our lives.

Isn't that wonderful? This means that the God none of us has ever seen is revealed in us if we truly love each other. And you, Laura and Ash, it means that the unseen God is especially to be revealed in the love between those committed to one another in marriage, for on this earth we are given this amazing opportunity to see the expression of divine love within the love of those committed to one another, as you are.

Isn't that awesome? When people who know nothing about the love of God for themselves look at us, our partnerships, our family life, our churches – in all their messiness and brokenness - they may then glimpse something of the love of God alive in us.

Laura and Ash, none of us has ever seen God. Yet, our prayer is that when, in days to come, we look at your marriage and your family life, people will see and believe in the all-loving but invisible God.

God is love and he wants us to be like him – to be loving people. His love is brought to completion; it is perfected; it is made whole, when it is displayed in our homes, our relationships, our churches. Don't forget this, Ash and Laura. By loving each other for the rest of your lives, the love of God is made complete in you.

Yet what exactly is meant by love in John's letter here? What is this love that we are to display?

Firstly, it is a love shown by giving. This love seeks to give rather than to get. It is a love which gladly and willingly makes sacrifices for the other. Love keeps on loving even when the other person finds it hard to respond; love keeps on loving without insisting upon anything in return. And, as well as being characterized by giving, it is marked by forgiving – making allowances for the fact that none of us is perfect and we all make mistakes.

It is a love shown by seeking: hoping and working for the good of the other person. It strives, to the very utmost, to avoid anything which is harmful, offensive, abusive or demeaning to the other. Within the marriage partnership this love means that neither partner must belittle each other nor subject one another to unkind behaviour.

It is a turning love, turning the heart towards the other and away from ourselves. But the self is never the only centre of the Christian's being. The gospel teaches us to always consider the happiness and feelings of others.

Of course, only one person has ever succeeded in truly giving over themself for the sake of others. Only One has ever succeeded in perfectly showing this pure love: that is Jesus. John says *'This is the kind of love we are talking about—not that we once upon a time loved God, but that he loved us and sent his Son as a sacrifice to clear away our sins and the damage they've done to our relationship with God.'* *'We love,'* says John in another place, *'because he first loved us'*.

Laura and Ash, how we rejoice with you and for you that God has joined you together. From this day on, you go down life's pathway together. As you do, remember the words of your wedding text: *No one has seen God, ever. But if we love one another, God dwells deeply within us, and his love becomes complete in us.*

Amen.

* * ♦ * *

I think I shocked a church member when one day, in an unguarded moment, I truthfully said something that might have been very hard to hear: 'I would much rather celebrate a funeral than a wedding.' At face value that is quite a bizarre thing to say. It is true that I have found it a privilege over the years to have been entrusted to lead funeral services for families at a time when they are at their most vulnerable. In our Baptist church communities, ministers tend to take the funerals of people that they know, in contrast to the sterling work done by our Anglican and Catholic colleagues, who are often called upon to lead funerals for strangers who live within their parish. It is also true that with a funeral the main client is less inclined to be argumentative or too opinionated.

What I meant by that unguarded comment was that, while it is undoubtedly a very joyful thing and a great privilege to be called upon to prepare couples to make their marriage vows and then to celebrate their commitment in the public declaration, there is a tremendous pressure for the special day to live up to the perfection and expense dedicated to weddings nowadays.

I also keep in mind the sobering statistic that some of the marriages I have conducted have ultimately failed - for all sorts of reasons and without the heavy hint of blame which people of faith can sometimes be prone to assign.

In 2021 my wife and I celebrated our ruby wedding – that is our 40th anniversary. With our previous church we celebrated our 25th wedding anniversary in 2006 with the renewal of vows. Around 150 guests joined us for a celebration meal afterwards. Our 40th was a much more low-key celebration, partly because of Covid, but it is a major milestone. We have made it to 40 plus years together. I am sure that there are many ways in which we are an oddity to our neighbours and to younger generations. One way in which we are distinctly odd in a society where relationships fracture much more frequently than one might hope is that we remain a strong partnership. Why might that be?

I have a respected colleague who when he speaks on the subject of marriage describes it as 'hard work'. I think that there is real truth in that, though there is also a healthy dose of what Christians call grace (and others might call good fortune). There is the whole process of learning how to live together in a way that doesn't crush but enhance. Also learning how to disagree in a way that doesn't close down relationships but ultimately strengthens them, drawing upon our different strengths and allowing the other to compensate for areas where we are less strong. And yes, in all of these much grace is very much needed.

A song that I listen to sometimes when I am out driving contains the lyric 'any loving is good loving.' Of course hearing such a line might sound alarm bells in the minds of those who like to police relationships, but I want to affirm it. I do indeed think that any loving is good loving. It all depends on what we mean by loving.

What I suspect the songwriter meant is that any kind of warm and positive encounter between human beings, particularly sexual, is good. What loving means to me is, I hope, an echo of what the writers of the New Testament intended their use of the word to mean. To love is to be committed to the well-being of someone else, choosing when necessary to put someone else's well-being ahead of your own (though avoiding an unhealthy imbalance in this). So, to truly love someone is to want to see them flourish as the person that they are, helping them to overcome the obstacles that confront them on their life's journey. It also means allowing them to be committed to your well-being and helping you surmount the boulders in your path too. All of this is underpinned and held secure by a promise of enduring commitment. That can indeed be hard work.

What I tried to say in the marriage homily above is that, in this world, it is very hard for us to make a difference or to stand up against some of the selfishness and self-centeredness that commonly prevails around us. Even if we think it will never be noticed or could possibly make the slightest difference, commitment and love call out, quietly and without a great show, that there is another way to live. Not everything need be drenched in cynicism or self-centredness.

No one has seen God, ever. But if we love one another, God dwells deeply within us, and his love becomes complete in us.

* * ♦ * *

CITY CONGREGATION

It was a cold, grey day in December and some people aged in their 80s were wearing two overcoats to keep warm.

Atop the stone steps into the church opposite the park, the multi-ethnic, multi-generational congregation made their way inside to worship. As usual the feeble heating made no noticeable difference. Glancing across a room of people singing heartily, I saw clouds of vapour billowing in front of their lips. There were more than 150 people standing among the sanctuary pews but they were dwarfed by the height of the room. During one hymn I saw two of the elders focus their binoculars on the ceiling, where a new crack in the Grade II listed plaster had appeared since the service had begun. Just another day at your church, then.

The famous Baptist preacher Charles Spurgeon had been asked to come and see the building after it was finished. When he got there, the Victorian prince of preachers - who was not shy to share his opinions - had said how much he disliked your building. This was more than a hundred years ago, so no-one alive could remember the specific criticisms about the architecture that had annoyed the great man. They probably included the acoustics since they had been a recurrent problem over the years. Without a sound system, it was hard to hear a speaker in some parts of the room. But that was nothing!

When I first visited your church I was shown around every room in the building, including the one that no one was allowed to enter as it was too unsafe. I have seen church towers and steeples that are shaky and some church stairs that have holes in them. But this was the first time I ever heard of a church room that was too risky to go into. It was a dangerous combination of rainwater and electricity. Soon, other rooms became off-limits too. Every time I visited, it seemed that another room was added to that list.

This was not a small or isolated church: both the congregation and the building were impressive. Nor was this one of those fading relics of faith where the wall plaques celebrated the past and the names of the long gone. It had some of those, of course, but this was a lively, faithful and growing congregation. They would come every Sunday, and sometimes during the week, to a building that was built as a towering display of power for Victorian nonconformity. It was much too big even then in more religious days for the numbers attending. Its splendour was mainly meant to compete with the Anglicans and Methodists in their own stone fortresses.

The tall, late-Victorian townhouses across the street and around the edge of the park were in that transition between old-fashioned elegance, multiple occupancy and emerging renovation. Families crammed into one or two rooms could feel the bracing breeze of Agas, tagines and stripped-pine blowing firmly down the road. This was one of the largest and poorest Baptist congregations in London. The overwhelming pastoral and social needs were a heavy burden: too heavy for two pastors in a row who both struggled emotionally. They kept going out of love for the people and for God; it was a love that was returned in full measure. But the stress of daily life was relentless.

A building like this – a Baptist basilica! – often tends to be a millstone for a poor congregation. Worse than that, one of those beloved inspectors who exist to protect old buildings had gone and chiseled the legend 'Grade II listed' into the millstone. So even if they had had the money (if…), any repairs and renewals would have had to weather the scrutiny of Listed Building Consent and the interference of The Victorian Society.

So we started working together, you and I. After I had seen every room in the building, including the one that was off-limits, we sat down to figure out how a church with no money could take care of a Grade II listed and increasingly run-down building. There were only a few options that we counted off on our fingers. The easiest solution was to send all the keys by recorded delivery to the Property Board. Let the guys in suits deal with the big problem! But we didn't have the heart to take that easy way out.

In front of your building, there was a concrete obstacle in the road, placed there by the council to stop joy-riders. But it didn't stop the first drive-by shooting that happened a week or two before. I had taken the train across east London that first day. When I left the building to walk back to the station, a group of leaders and other muscular guys walked with me as an escort. They thought a former librarian with glasses might be an easy target. That was the last time I visited you by train.

So no, we did not lock the doors and send the keys back. Over the next year and a half you - the congregation – patiently prayed and trusted and asked questions of the key movers, shakers and decision makers in your neighbourhood. We asked what the church might do to make the greatest difference to the quality of life in the community and how its building might underpin that work. We talked to headteachers and GPs; to neighbours and friends and shopkeepers. Then we thought and prayed some more. Our conversations were often in the evenings after work and so we ordered-in pizza. The delivery drivers were reluctant to visit that part of town. Even when they arrived, they had never brought pizza to a church before and stood amazed at it all. We laughed and cried together. We dreamed and hoped. We prayed and ate pizza.

It seems to me that when a solution to an

intractable problem appears, you say your thank-yous both loudly and softly. Loudly, thanking God; together softly and humbly, grateful that you have not faced the awful alternatives. For we knew that any solution owed all to grace and less to our efforts. When you celebrate what has been done among you, but not by you, you acknowledge that the solution is for this season alone. The future will bring new challenges and a different team will need to rise to meet them.

I know some readers might be eager to hear how we found that magic bullet, you and I. There are many faithful groups in similar buildings around the UK who face the same problems that we did. But the truth is that there was no amazing and surprising solution, given to us by a hidden hand (though I have seen that happen in other cases and places). Instead, it was the process of listening to God's mission, to what he was already doing in his great love for those who lived around the church, through the insights shared by key workers and residents, that your focus gradually shifted from the building's problems to the people close by. For in every neighbourhood, miracles can happen when people are noticed, welcomed, included and loved for who they are.

Though we had no name for it at the time, we took the road of 'missional listening'. That is for those who know they are called to a place and people but do not yet know what that means in practice. You pay attention to God and to the community at the same time, to discover what God is already doing and where we can join in.

We changed, together. You took me to your hearts and allowed me to talk up some possibilities. I think you probably knew that I was putting on a confident face. Something happens, sometimes, when we meet together acknowledging our helplessness in the face of circumstance and just ask God to find a way. This time, he did. Today your church and building are thriving. More people; new people. The church has a new name. The heating works. You are shouldering that millstone well.

* * ♦ * *

I know everything you have done, including your hard work and how you have endured…You have endured and gone through hard times because of me, yet you have not given up. But I do have something against you! And it is this: you don't have as much love as you used to. Revelation 2: 2-3

Picture a town full of every nationality and culture. Different languages can be heard spoken on each street corner.

Imagine large numbers of people travelling into and out of the city each day. There are many shops and alongside the shops there are street traders calling out to the passers-by. It is crowded and there is much jostling. Heavy traffic pushes along the roads; some of it passenger transport and the rest goods for the shops or food and drink for the pubs. On many of the streets you see buildings dedicated to different religions. Some have lots of people going in and out of them; others only a few. One of the things you notice as you go into this town is that some of the women, and not a few men too, show off their bodies in ways that catch the eye.

In one part of town you come to a large public hall, hired for the evening. It is summertime: as darkness begins to fall there remains a stifling heat. The noise of the street traders continues all around. You look through the windows and inside you see a group of people singing and praying. This is a church, gathered for worship after many of them have stopped work late, after an exhausting day in the heat.

Just look at the people inside. There are folk in that hall from all over the world. Written into the lines of their faces is the long story of a faith held against hardship. Of perseverance. Of holding on when there is nothing left except the determination to stand firm regardless. Because as a church they have been through it. They've had their disagreements. Their leaders may have been a disappointment. Some church members have spoken harshly about one another. The church has been a magnet for the weird and whacky, some of whose poison has infected easily-led people. At their core, even those who have worked hard, persevered and held on feel dog-tired. They look back on all the years they have been part of that church and they know that once they were on fire for God. All that now remains are the embers of the fire that all but died out years ago. They still meet. They remember the old songs; but no new songs come. The unspoken fear is that, without some new encounter with God's Spirit, the pressure of life in the town and the daily gains made by the other religions will soon snuff out the last flicker of the flame that once burned bright and the church there will die.

It would be unfair to ask you if you know that church. I could take you to many such, in many towns and cities. Maybe there are aspects of your church which came to mind as you read these words. Yet the word picture I have drawn for you today is of the church in Ephesus around 90AD, when God inspired a writer called John to set down words we find in The Book of Revelation, chapter 2.

And that is the last mention we have in the Bible of the great church at Ephesus. Established by the apostle Paul, who stumbled across a group of lost and confused disciples there when he first visited about 19-20 years after the resurrection of Jesus. These folk had understood and confronted their brokenness and wrongdoing. Determined to live differently, they had been baptised by the disciples of John the Baptist. Paul spent time there, teaching them the truth about the gospel and he then baptised them as followers of Jesus. God, who had already been at work in them – preparing them – then filled them with both love and the strength to live differently.

Paul lived at the house of Priscilla and her husband Aquila who were Jewish tentmakers and pioneer leaders. When he moved on, Paul left the church in their care. The ancient world was male-centred and knew nothing of the Victorian politeness of 'ladies first'. It is possible that the only reason why the Bible - several times – records the wife's name ahead of her husband's is that Priscilla had a greater responsibility than her husband. Or that both were elders and she was the leading elder of the church there. Again from the biblical account we know that to Priscilla and Aquila (once again in that order) was also entrusted the instruction of others like Apollos – a gifted teacher. Priscilla and Aquila were forced to leave after the riots mentioned in the Book of Acts but they later returned to lead the church alongside Paul's personal representative and adopted son, Timothy.

Timothy was close personally to Paul, through whom he had come to trust in Jesus. Like many others, he had known the tension of being in a family where half were believers and the other half not-yet-believers. Also the experience of being of mixed-ethnicity. He was a younger man, to whom great responsibility was given in the church and who may have felt nervous and uncertain when he had to make tough decisions.

What might any of this have to do with us? Although all of this took place in the latter years of the 1st century AD, I am struck by the similarities between Ephesus and Southend-on-Sea, the UK city in which I live. I see the competition between religions and the pressure in the church to hold on to the faith they first received. I feel the testimony of a church struggling with a prevailing culture dominated by sexuality without boundaries, by money and by doctrinal purity - insistence not only on being 'right' but acknowledged as such. I know many churches made up of Christians who work hard, persevere and continue in their quiet witness but among whom are some whose first love for Christ has dimmed over the years, to be replaced by the habits of religion.

Later in the New Testament we find a letter written to Timothy (we call this letter 1 Timothy) setting out Paul's great love for his adopted son and into whose care he has passed a church which he led for nearly 3 years. In that letter he says:

"I'm passing this work on to you, my son Timothy. The prophetic word that was directed to you prepared us for this. All those prayers are coming together now so you will do this well, fearless in your struggle, keeping a firm grip on your faith and on yourself. After all, this is a fight we're in. There are some, you know, who by relaxing their grip and thinking anything goes have made a thorough mess of their faith.   1 Timothy 1:18-19

The life of faith is sometimes a struggle. When life's difficulties come along, so many of us duck down and hope they will go away, avoiding facing up to them. If we don't face our troubles, one way or another they tend to come back stronger next time. Yet if, with God's help, we do face them – though we may feel weak - we are the stronger when the next problem comes along.

Make no mistake. *"In the world you will have trouble,"* said Jesus. Hoping that somehow it will all go away, we may find that we are at the mercy of whatever is blown in our direction. There are systemic powers at work in this world whose aim is not merely the frustration of good but its destruction. It is in this context that Paul encourages us, just as he encourages Timothy and the Ephesian Christians to fight! Let's not become like the church at Ephesus – one where, weary of the good fight, we lose our first love of God. In spite of all discouragements, we are called to fight on.

* * ♦ * *

ANNETTE AND JACK

Each morning I would turn the corner and walk by your house on my way to Wix's Lane Junior School. I would greet you and smile if you were outside, and you would do the same. But I knew you better from the church across the street from our house. For you were the leaders of the Sunday School at the Congregational Church.

Our weekends in the 1960s seemed to run on a routine. Dad would take us to Clapham Junction on Saturday mornings, down the road from Lavender Hill, to shop a bit and let Mum have some time off (she was with us all week). We would stroll through the market on Northcote Road, which was a real, bustling market back then, not the fancy one with Aga stoves, olive oil and lattes that it is today. Sometimes, we would get a treat at Joe Lyons, like a hot blackcurrant drink or a milkshake. In the afternoon, Dad would press his clothes for work next week and we would either watch TV or play outside on the street.

Mum and Dad wanted to sleep-in on Sunday mornings, but that was hard to do with two young kids. That's why they sent us to the Sunday School across the street, even though they were both atheists who had sometimes plotted to overthrow the government. Mum would always say that she hoped it would make us immune to religion, but I think they just wanted some peace, quiet and time together (and who could blame them?).

Life was very different then. Adults looked so very old. In sharp contrast to today, when people of 70 or 80 years of age make every effort to appear youthful, in those days as soon as they turned 21 many men would adopt a drab, dust-coloured raincoat and most would have a short back and sides haircut. Another difference was that, in those days, a great many children went to Sunday School. They were well-attended and so you might make new friends, as well as those you played with in the street or from school.

I do not remember very much of the content of the Sunday school. We sang and listened to stories from the Old Testament. All the major stories of the Bible were better known then, including the stories of Jesus. Everyone had to sit still and listen. You had sons of your own and knew how to keep order in a large group of kids. There was more deference then: was that such a bad thing?

As I look back now, I see something in your dedication to running the Sunday school that I have encountered in many different places over the years since. Some people spent their spare time playing or watching sport; down at the pub or in the garden. You, however, were those rare folk who give their time and energy so faithfully and sacrificially to making something work that, without all that dedication, would just never happen. You were there week after week, patiently showing love and kindness and teaching kids to read better, from the hymn book and the Bible.

I wonder sometimes what fruit you saw from all that work?

There was a painted, cast-iron pointing finger sign up at the top of the road that said 'To Congregational the Church'. It was only later that I realised that the text was in two columns, which made a little more sense. No 17, where we lived, was demolished soon after 1968. It had four storeys, columns by the lemon yellow front door and a commanding façade that was able to look the Victorian church opposite in the eye. In time it was replaced by a rabbit hutch of a house: a reduction in the housing capacity that the compulsory purchase order was supposedly intended to rectify. The church building was also demolished, to be replaced by another that looks today like a redundant health centre in a postwar new town. Perhaps that isn't so bad. A church should be a hospital for sick souls. By then, of course, we had moved as a family a little further around south London to Tooting.

There, too, we found more people like you but with other names. People whose dedicated service is rarely acknowledged and who do not tend to make it into the history books but who have shaped the histories of countless people in such positive and affirming ways.

Thank you loving God for all those who, without clamouring for recognition or attention, so quietly and lovingly give their time, energy and God-given abilities to help to shape us as people who will, in turn, learn to love. May their experience of cheerful service be rewarded with satisfaction in life and the knowledge that they are co-workers with you. For those that rest now from their life's work we thank you again, gracious God.

* * ♦ * *

Walking along the beach of Lake Galilee, Jesus saw two brothers: Simon (later called Peter) and Andrew. They were fishing, throwing their nets into the lake. It was their regular work. Jesus said to them, "Come with me. I'll make a new kind of fisherman out of you. I'll show you how to catch men and women instead of perch and bass." They didn't ask questions, but simply dropped their nets and followed.

A short distance down the beach they came upon another pair of brothers, James and John, Zebedee's sons. These two were sitting in a boat with their father, Zebedee, mending their fishnets. Jesus made the same offer to them, and they were just as quick to follow, abandoning boat and father. Matthew 4: 18-22

You might have to recall long distant memories for this. Imagine you are back in your school/college class. You are lost in your thoughts as usual; the lesson is boring. Then another teacher comes in and starts talking to the class. This one is new to the school and teaches the subject you love. You enjoy her classes because they are fun and interesting and you like her as a person and a teacher. You know you can learn a lot from her. Suddenly she says to the class "Let's go, everyone, let's go! Come with me on an learning adventure, a new beginning for your life. Let's leave this place and do some real learning. You have to give up everything if you want to come with me. I don't know what will happen but it will be worth it. This will be something new: a life you never dreamed of. It's a clear choice: go or stay. So who wants that? Who's coming with me?"

Well, what would you do?

Jesus spent his time on earth calling and training followers, forming them into a community that trusted him and lived his way. In the Jewish culture of the first century, the rabbi asked disciples to not only learn facts but to also share life with the teacher, absorbing his values and shaping their lives after his. Being with Jesus and learning from him was enough to change their world completely. It was the disciples that Jesus invited that became the first church.

Some of you who are reading this are already followers of Jesus: what do we think we have agreed to? Is that what you wanted when you heard Jesus calling you to go with him?

In this story, Jesus invites his first few disciples and they join him to be his followers. They agree to a new way of life and commit to it. So what did they think following Jesus meant? The first thing is clear, but needs to be said. They decide to follow Jesus. To go with Jesus. Physically. To walk away with him. They literally followed him, going where he went. That is difficult for us to do today since Jesus is not here with us in the same way. We cannot physically leave our life as we know it and go travelling with him. But what they were doing by following him was becoming his students; his learners; his disciples.

'Disciple' is a word that is only used in the Christian context in modern English. Now, we might say 'apprentice'. They agreed to an apprenticeship with Jesus. Maybe you were an apprentice when you were young? But let's not think of apprentices as we see them on Lord Sugar's show! What does it really mean that the disciples were Jesus's apprentices? It means they were physically with him, observing how he lived and listening to what he said. They wanted to learn how to answer their question: how do I live / think / speak / act as if Jesus is now living in me? How would Jesus behave if he had my family, my income, my job, my home, my illness, my joys and my worries - what would he do? How would his choices and values change my life?

That is what it looks like to follow Jesus. We follow him. We sign-up for an apprenticeship with Jesus. We look at his teaching, we look at his life, we read the Bible – which was central to his life too – and we ask: how is my life to be different now if Christ is living in me?

The second thing that happens when someone agrees to follow Jesus is that choice affects everything else. Did you notice that when the gospel writer tells us these fishermen followed Jesus, he emphasizes what they left behind? He says that 'They left their nets at once and followed him.' And again, 'They immediately left the boat and their father and followed him.' To follow Jesus they had to leave behind their nets, their boat and their parents. Their nets and boat were their source of income, in a culture without any social security. Their father was the leader of their family, who deserved their loyalty and respect. Yet Jesus had to become more important than their family and the culture that shaped that duty. More important for them than their job and the way to support their families. It wasn't just these fishermen who might have been in this together. Levi, in the story in Luke's gospel, walked away from his profitable, but morally questionable, business.

Now we aren't them. Jesus was calling them, quite literally, to follow him wherever he went. That meant they had to hand in their notice and go. We're not in their position. In fact, it would be wrong for most of us to leave our families or simply to resign from our jobs or caring responsibility. Jesus explains later on that we must not use following God as an excuse to avoid caring for our families. The rest of the Bible is clear that we need to work if we can, so that we can provide for ourselves and have something left over for those in need.

But let's not avoid the main point here. Jesus calls

us today to put his life and values before everything else. That is not to disrespect our family or other commitments. It is only when we put God's way first that we see all the other parts of our lives in their true perspective. That is hard for us to hear. This makes the call to be an apprentice of Jesus something quite different. Not to be just churchgoers or to be 'spiritual'. Instead we must ask: what is life like if lived according to the values and choices of Jesus do? That needs to guide the whole of our lives.

Following Jesus for these fishermen meant a change of direction and purpose in their lives. Those we read about in Matthew's gospel above were fishermen. Jesus calls them to go fishing for people. What did he mean? Well, the rest of the gospel story makes clear that they were to help others to find and follow Jesus. To make disciples is to help others to find and follow Jesus for themselves.

Wouldn't it be much easier for us if Jesus had just said "Come with me" and not given us the job of sharing news of him with others? If following Jesus was just a personal matter. For one thing, we Christians might be more accepted in society rather than often being seen as annoying weirdos. Many people are fine with us being Christians as long as we keep what we believe to ourselves. Yet Jesus calls us to be fishers of people. He is not telling us to do this in any specific way. He is not saying we have to use a megaphone or bother people in the street or push gospel leaflets into people's hands in

Sainsbury's. He is simply saying that the good news he came to bring is too good to keep to ourselves.

Come with me, says Jesus. If I am your Teacher, I must come first – it's my life you are living; my values you are to live by. Don't keep me all to yourselves: share me with others. Jesus is the person God sent into our world for our good. He calls us to follow him; to let him take first place and to fish for others.

That's the gospel. That's the good news about God. That's what we sign-up for.

* * ♦ * *

BRIDGET

On Saturday nights in term time, the centre of the City of Brighton buzzes with students at gigs, on pub crawls and just hanging out. That is as true today as it was late on a Saturday night there in 1980.

In those student days, Saturday evenings were so often an opportunity to have an early evening burger in town and then to catch a movie. Sometimes we might finish the evening in the 'King and Queen', the student pub in the centre of the city (and yes, we could afford it all on the full student grants denied now to our children). Nikki lived in Grove Street off Albion Hill, one of those steep climbs from the Old Steine up towards the back streets of Kemp Town. She and I would walk back to her digs together, taking the incline at a steady pace before a lingering farewell. Then I would walk back down the hill, crossing the road, the grass and the other carriageway beyond, before making another ascent up the ill-lit Trafalgar Street towards the station. The last bus that would take me to my own digs at the far end of Hove needed to be caught outside the station, otherwise it would be a long walk home.

When you make the same journey so many times, it is easy to slip into a mental autopilot, mesmerized by the pounding of feet on pavement. It was less common then to have the same background fear that seems to haunt night-time urban walks nowadays. Almost at the foot of Grove Hill I was startled out of my reverie by voice that simply said: 'Can you please help me?'

You were leaning on a low wall. An older woman. How old were you? So hard to tell in those days. This was before the emergence of perpetual youthfulness among seniors. Older women then often had old-lady perms. You were certainly older than my mother but perhaps not quite as old as my nan.

'What can I do?' I asked. 'See me home, dear,' you replied. 'I've had a drop to drink. I don't live far but I don't think I'm going to make it without help.'

The middle-aged man of 2024 watches all this with amazement. You cannot be serious! A 20-year-old man and a vulnerable woman – at best tipsy – alone and in the dark? But the klaxons sounding now as I recall a night over 40 years ago are those of today's safeguarding age. Nowadays any kind of situation can seem threatening. Everyday happenings that, in our childhood and youth, would have just seemed unremarkable would today be shot through with looming risk.

And so you took my arm, gathered your strength and your handbag and stood up. We turned in the direction of your home. We pigeon-stepped up the foothills of Grove Hill, our speed regulated not only by the incline but also by size 5 feet and too many port-and-lemons.

When we reached your front door, you handed me your Yale key and we soon had the door open. 'Come in' you said. The safeguarding alarms of the 21st century are now deafening but, on that night, there was simply silence broken by the swinging open of your sitting room door and the swish of feet on carpet. You sat down on the sofa. I checked you were OK. You thanked me but, to be honest, you were half-asleep within a minute of being home. So I let myself out, closing the front door quietly so as not to disturb. Then back (again!) down the hill but by then too late for the last bus home to Hove. Therefore, an hour's walk through the empty streets.

Did we introduce ourselves? I don't recall. So, not knowing your name (please forgive me if I take a liberty here) I have named you Bridget. I don't know why precisely. Maybe I caught an Irish lilt to your voice and you were of the right generation for Bridgets. It doesn't matter. It is enough that names confer some dignity and respect.

Was I foolish to walk you into your home, alone? Possibly. Innocent, certainly. But that is one of those first remembered occasions when I came to understand something about myself — the desire to be helpful. To make a difference. The only witnesses to that once-only Saturday night meeting and our conversation were the silent Observer and his company who look upon us all with an unwavering gaze of love. My public telling of this tale may have blown a chunk of my credit with him! But Bridget, though you would never know, our unexpected encounter helped to shape me and to steer the direction of my life.

* * ♦ * *

He got up from the supper table, set aside his robe, and put on an apron. Then he poured water into a basin and began to wash the feet of the disciples, drying them with his apron. When he got to Simon Peter, Peter said, "Master, you wash my feet?" Jesus answered, "You don't understand now what I'm doing, but it will be clear enough to you later." Peter persisted, "You're not going to wash my feet—ever!" Jesus said, "If I don't wash you, you can't be part of what I'm doing."

"Master!" said Peter. "Not only my feet, then. Wash my hands! Wash my head!" Jesus said, "If you've had a bath in the morning, you only need your feet washed now and you're clean from head to toe. My concern, you understand, is holiness, not hygiene. So now you're clean…. After he had finished washing their feet, he took his robe, put it back on, and went back to his place at the table. Then he said, "Do you understand what I have done to you? You address me as 'Teacher' and 'Master,' and rightly so. That is what I am. So if I, the Master and Teacher, washed your feet, you must now wash each other's feet. I've laid down a pattern for you. What I've done, you do. I'm only pointing out the obvious. A servant is not ranked above his master; an employee doesn't give orders to the

employer. If you understand what I'm telling you, act like it—and live a blessed life. John 13: 1-17

The essence of Jesus' teachings that I have learned and adopted as a guide for my life is this: *'If you understand what I am telling you, act like it – and live a blessed life.'* Or, as another way of saying the same thing: *'Now that you know these things, you will be blessed if you do them.'* I believe that faith should seek understanding. Yet the true measure of our lives is not how precise our theology is, but whether we have served others in humble ways, such as washing feet, giving water to the thirsty and spending time with those who are sick or imprisoned by their circumstances.

And the same is true for you, reader. Now that you know these things, you also will be blessed if you do them too.

* * ♦ * *

MR & MRS LANE

We were still in the first few years of married life and you were in the last few years of your long partnership. We first met you when you appeared one week at the small homegroup that we were part of, just around the corner from our house. So quietly spoken, Mr Lane you were always well-dressed in a three-piece suit, which is not surprising as you had been a tailor's cutter working in a bespoke gentlemen's tailors in Savile Row. You were plainly devoted still to Mrs Lane after so many years together. That devotion was returned in full measure. Principally, I think, it was in the gentle ways in which you looked at one another and the smile when the other spoke.

After a while getting to know the folk in this new church group you had joined out of the blue, you did what people often used to do in those days and sadly do far less now. You invited this young couple to Sunday lunch. So it was that we came to your flat and you made us very much at home. The table was set and we were treated as honoured guests. I suspect looking back that that meal gave you just as much pleasure to host as it gave us to enjoy with you. You both served as hosts with the practiced moves of a team that had been together for half a century.

It was there that we heard some of the secrets of your long and happy marriage. You explained it to us, Mrs Lane. You said that there were always going to be arguments and disagreements when you're married and that an awful lot of them would be about things that didn't matter very much. For example, who had misplaced a piece of paper, a kitchen implement or any household item. All such disagreements could be a flashpoint. So, instead of saying to one another: 'You've gone and lost such and such', you had evolved the habit of saying that any issue would always be the fault of 'someone'.

'Someone's gone and lost the nutcrackers,' one of you would say. 'Really? I don't know who would have done that.' And because the loss had been caused by a third party, you could then both join in the search for the missing item without it becoming a serious risk of disagreement and hurt.

Forty years later, we still sometimes find ourselves saying: 'Someone's gone and lost the....' We learned that from you, Mr & Mrs Lane. Your tenderness and commitment to one another was evident in all you did and said. You had such a loving partnership together for so many decades. When one died, the other followed a short time later. Together in life; not wanting to be parted in death.

Thank goodness that 'Someone' introduced us to you and gave us that glimpse into how a loving relationship works over the long distance.

* * ♦ * *

Do you see what this means—all these pioneers who blazed the way, all these veterans cheering us on? It means we'd better get on with it. Hebrews 12: 1

Each November in the Christian calendar we have the feast of All Saints. Thinking about saints is Christian. Historically, Baptist Christians have been a bit sniffy about that because of some other traditions' focus upon saints as an alternative conduit to God. Yet, for countless generations, Christians have repeated the words of the Apostles' creed: 'I believe in… …the communion of saints." So what is it that we believe in? Who are the saints with whom we are in communion? The world around us – if it thinks of saints at all – thinks of good people: Mother Theresa, for example. Others use the word 'saint' as a title of honour for those whose lives have demonstrated exemplary goodness.

I think that the communion of saints is about our being part of the body of believers, past, present and future, who confess their faith in Christ. If you could see the church of God throughout the ages, it would be an amazing sight. A few famous people but the vast majority in that crowd are ordinary folk, like you and me, who have placed their trust in Jesus, with his help, and made it their business to love God and their neighbours both. Even more amazing would be the realization that you and I have our places there within that great gathering of the faithful.

All Saints' Day on 1st November reminds us of being part of 'that great cloud of witnesses' as the author of the biblical Letter to the Hebrews puts it. We are part of that immense multitude of people following his call and with our spiritual DNA now, slowly, being re-coded to be identical with that of Christ.

"*All these pioneers who blazed the way, all these veterans cheering us on*" says our text. Our spectators are the Old Testament heroes of faith: Abel, Enoch, Noah, Abraham, Isaac, Jacob, Joseph, the parents of Moses, Moses, the people of Israel, the prostitute Rahab, Gideon, Samson, Jephthah, Ruth, David, Samuel, Esther, and the prophets. They cheer us on to run the race of life by faith, spurring us on to greater efforts.

And in that mighty company are so many who, by the standards of their time, had little fame and no renown: the Mr & Mrs Lanes and countless others like them. Daughters and sons of God who, in their gentleness, love and dedication, showed glimmers of Christlikeness in their characters and actions.

So today, I remember with gratitude those whose good examples remind me of what I can be at my best.

Perhaps also the stories of their lives may remind all of us of who we are; the one in whom we believe and what, with his help, we may become.

* * ♦ * *

VELMA
on the occasion of your baptism

I thank you, High God—you're breathtaking! Body and soul, I am marvellously made! I worship in adoration—what a creation! You know me inside and out, you know every bone in my body; you know exactly how I was made, bit by bit, how I was sculpted from nothing into something. Psalm 139 v 14

Was the Psalm writer correct when he said that? Or do you think that we're just a mixture of chemicals? As Professor Joad of the Brains Trust once famously said:

'Man is nothing but

Fat enough for seven bars of soap

Iron enough for one medium sized nail

Sugar enough for 7 cups of tea

Lime enough to whitewash a chicken coop

Phosphorous enough to tip 2,200 matches

Magnesium enough for one dose of salts

Potash enough to explode one toy crane

Sulphur enough to rid one dog of fleas'. [viii]

Well that might describe the chemical ingredients of our bodies but it is neither nice nor very uplifting, is it? Nor does it describe the whole story. Far from it. So, as well as being more poetic, the biblical account is much affirming: *'I was sculpted from nothing into something.'* It speaks of intent, not just ingredients. Praise of God is a good response for us human beings, offered to the Creator and the Giver of life. Today we meet to celebrate the fact that, marvellously, God continues to grow and develop our characters, to become like his.

Velma, you come here to this church week by week to share in our praise of God and to thank him, for you have come to realise that you and your son are marvellously and wonderfully made. And this morning, as we have all seen today, you came here to be baptised. But what is baptism?

In all kinds of ways we humans use signs to stand for things that have significance for us. These are visible expressions of something that is difficult to put into words. A kiss shows love; a handshake shows friendship; a salute shows loyalty and at a wedding we give and receive rings, which are signs of commitment. For us, baptism shows that we now choose to identify ourselves as belonging to Christ and are received into his church. That sense of 'belonging' can be life-enhancing: to know we are loved by God and that we are precious to him. We now join the company of others who share that knowledge and experience.

Velma, you are unique, just as we all are. There is

no one else exactly like you in the whole world. The word unique means 'being only of one kind; being without equal'. Yet we often forget this. We remind ourselves of our brokenness and that life's experiences often spoil, stain or mess up the loveliness that God made us to be. And that happens to us all. That is why in baptism we use water as a sign of cleansing. It is a bath to symbolize the washing away of the past with all its wrongdoing. None of us, though wonderfully made, is perfect.

Baptism signifies a great change of direction in our lives, away from both honest mistakes made and also for when we have deliberately made wrong choices that hurt us, others and God too. It shows that we recognise our need for forgiveness. That is why the baptism service includes questions for the candidate to answer: 'Do you turn to Christ? Do you repent of your sins?'

Baptism marks a new start. From this point on, we must make every effort to avoid returning to the old ways of living that led us to a dead end. Now, with God's help, we do all we can to know the difference between right and wrong and to set others a good example. This isn't just a self-help method. The good news about Jesus is that God, recognising that we cannot help ourselves, has made a new way of life possible through his Son. We can now live a different life because he makes it possible.

That is not all. Through baptism we show that we are brought into the church family, not only of the local church, but of the Church worldwide and, indeed, of all times and places.

In a story found in the New Testament book of Acts, the jailer holding Christian church planters Paul and Silas captive asks:

"Sirs, what do I have to do to be saved, to really live?" They said, "Put your entire trust in the Master Jesus. Then you'll live as you were meant to live—and everyone in your house included!" They went on to spell out in detail the story of the Master—the entire family got in on this part. They never did get to bed that night. The jailer made them feel at home, dressed their wounds, and then—he couldn't wait till morning!—was baptized, he and everyone in his family. There in his home, he had food set out for a festive meal. It was a night to remember: He and his entire family had put their trust in God; everyone in the house was in on the celebration. Acts 16: 31-34

Velma, different streams of the one church have different understandings about how and when baptism should take place. Today, however, you have been baptised not because someone told you to; not because it was a way to get into church as a community or club but because you chose to be obedient to the call of Jesus, whom you have come to follow for yourself.

Many people are christened as infants. It is indeed wonderful that their parents acknowledge the gift of their child with thanksgiving to God and we respect the traditions of our sister churches. Yet here today we celebrate that someone has freely chosen for themselves to make Christ's way theirs; to live by his values and to become like him. I hope that what has been seen and heard here today will help all of us to do just this ... and encourage us all to follow Christ day by day.

Does your baptism mean that you will be perfect from now on? No, Velma, you are still human like the rest of us and, like all of us, you will still make mistakes alongside all the good that we hope you will do. But we know that, for you, today is a turning point. From today you have said publicly, to your family and friends, that you now intend your life to move to a different beat.

You know me inside and out, you know every bone in my body; you know exactly how I was made, bit by bit, how I was sculpted from nothing into something.

Velma, today now starts the journey of your being remade in the image of God. We, your church family, will pray for you and be your companions as you take the next steps in the journey of faith.

* * ♦ * *

On the Sabbath, we left the city and went down along the river where we had heard there was to be a prayer meeting. We took our place with the women who had gathered there and talked with them. One woman, Lydia, was from Thyatira and a dealer in expensive [purple-dyed] textiles, known to be a God-fearing woman. As she listened with intensity to what was being said, the Master gave her a trusting heart—and she believed! After she was baptized, along with everyone in her household, she said in a surge of hospitality, "If you're confident that I'm in this with you and believe in the

Master truly, come home with me and be my guests." We hesitated, but she wouldn't take no for an answer. Acts 16:13-15

Written in more patriarchal times, a great many of the characters we find in the Bible – both heroes and villains – are men. The fewer women who are mentioned tend to be outstanding, usually in terms of their virtue, though Jezebel is perhaps the arch female villain in the Bible. Often female characters are unnamed – an injustice, considering that some stories pivot on their faith and faithfulness. I still think it important that the church should correct this injustice by finding an equal number of ways to honour all those women in our extended families and acquaintance who have loved us into well-being—whether we call them 'wife' or 'mother' or 'grandmother' or 'stepmother' or 'aunt' or 'sister' or 'partner' or 'daughter' or 'cousin' or 'granny' or 'friend' or 'teacher' or 'boss'.

In reflecting upon the example of godly women and of baptism, I am reminded of someone who drew on her resources – character and possessions – to love an early expression of church as it began and nurture its well-being. Lydia was a businesswoman who out of her generosity provided the meeting place for the first gathering of Christians, the first 'church', in the Greek city of Philippi. According to the account that we read in chapter 16 of the New Testament Book of Acts, Lydia is an early baptized follower of Jesus in Europe. She then hosts church gatherings and services in her home.

Lydia: the name is really rather interesting. It is the name of a geographic territory like *Paris* Hilton. Now, in Lydia's time, the people most likely to be named after a geographic area are not fiction heroes or glamorous movie stars but slaves, named after the place from which they've been taken. So Lydia might well have previously been a slave who came from the province in Asia Minor of the same name. Yet when Luke, the author of Acts, first introduces us to Lydia, she's living as a free woman in Macedonia—i.e., northern Greece—in the city of Philippi, a Roman military colony. In fact, she's now a prosperous householder who is a trader in purple-dyed cloth, a very expensive commodity favoured by the nobility. Lydia's trade is one known to have been practiced by a number of ex-slaves, and she has obviously proved to be successful at it.

Yet Lydia is far more than just a successful businesswoman. She has a strong spiritual side to her character as well. Amid a crowded field of potential gods and goddesses to worship, she is one of those gentiles who's been attracted to the one-God religion and ethics of Judaism. On the Jewish sabbath, she regularly gathers with others like her at a site about a mile west of town, along a local riverbank. Luke calls it "a place of prayer," by which he may mean an open-air place of worship used mainly by women, as the more formal buildings for worship may have been exclusively for men alone.

On one particular sabbath day, Lydia and other women at the place of prayer meet two Jewish men who've been announcing Jesus as the Messiah. They are the apostle Paul and his companion Silas. They've just arrived in Europe after their previous missionary work in Asia Minor. The women welcome Paul and Silas, and they invite Paul, as a visiting rabbi, to teach them. Paul, acting contrary to his cultural tradition, agrees to do so. Lydia listens eagerly to his teaching about Jesus and the message rings true to her. So right then and there, her heart is warmed and she accepts Jesus as the Messiah longed for by the Jews, whereupon she makes her life-changing choice and is baptized by Paul in that nearby river—she and her whole household. That probably means Lydia together with her children, extended family, employees and slaves. So here we see Lydia, the successful businesswoman, who is doubtless decisive in business, responding just as decisively when Paul offers her quite a radical change in her life's direction - to be a follower of Jesus.

Following Lydia's baptism, she urges Paul and Silas to accept the hospitality of her home for the duration of their stay in Philippi, and this home of hers swiftly becomes the local house-church, the place in which the developing Christian community gathers. People of both genders and of every social class and ethnic group are embraced and gathered together for the sharing of meals and resources and for the lively worship of God together. This is incredibly countercultural for that place and time.

So, this lady whose whole household is baptized alongside her, opens her home for nurturing the spiritual well-being of others and thereby becomes a mother-figure for every Christian in Philippi. Lydia puts into practice an inclusive hospitality, a welcome that flies in the face of the social conventions of her time. Through her, the good news of Christ's love begins the work of breaking down every barrier posed by gender, class or ethnicity. She joins the other examples of fine female leadership in the earliest churches, seen in the Bible and in other contemporary sources. It was only later that the importance of their roles and influence was displaced by male dominance. How many of us have been nurtured into growth as people – and as people of faith – by godly women like Lydia? Let us give grateful thanks for all those who have journeyed ahead of us through baptism and faithful following of Christ and whose example we may hope to imitate.

* * ♦ * *

Part Three

YOU AND ME

* * ♦ * *

NAMELESS

I have always had trouble remembering names, which is why I often call even those people I have known for a long time 'mate' or 'dear'. I have never had any such trouble with faces, though. When I go back to east London where we lived for 28 years, I sometimes see a familiar face across the street and think: I know you! Or at least I recognise your face. Did I ever know your name? And how did we know each other?

The problem in telling this story is that I have neither name nor face to go on. Actually I know nothing about you as a person, which is strange considering how you and your actions affected the lives of both my family and me. I don't know if you are male or female, old or young, tall or short. I don't know your culture or ethnicity. Given the many hundreds, maybe thousands of encounters we have with other human beings in our lifetimes, I suppose it is not so strange that in the crowd of personalities and strong emotions there might be one or two who come to hate us, to the point of wanting to hurt us.

It started with the tyres. In those days our car was a red Ford Sierra. We have sometimes named our cars and this one was Mabel. She was, if I recall, the car that we owned for the longest time of all of them. Mabel had the familiar jelly-mould style of body from the 1980s and 90s. Even after driving her for eight years it was hard to tell where the rear bumper was when reversing.

I still remember the first occasion when, driving along slowly, I could hear a click, click, click from the near side of the car. Pulling over out of the traffic, we found a long screw embedded in the front tyre. This was still holding its pressure and so we drove to a tyre shop and had it replaced – the depth of the puncture being too severe to repair. That was the first time.

Then, over the next few months, we found screws embedded in tyre after tyre. It became quite costly because not all of the punctures could be repaired. I didn't want to believe that this was anything more than an unfortunate set of coincidences. Then one day, as I prepared to reverse the car onto the road, I looked underneath. As usual I had parked on the hard standing at the front of the house. There, propped behind one of the tyres, was a screw waiting for me to reverse off the frontage, which would cause another immediate puncture.

Early in this book I told the story of Bruno, a Congolese friend whose asylum claim was declined and all appeals exhausted. When we found that he had been taken to Oakington detention centre, a few miles north of Cambridge, some of us obtained permission to visit him to encourage him as he awaited certain deportation.

He wanted to make sure that arrangements were in place to sort his finances and key possessions, so that these could be sent on to him later in the Republic of Congo. By then we had said farewell to Mable the Sierra and I set off ready to go up the M11 in our unnamed Peugeot 405. Just as the car picked up speed, a knocking sound began on the rear axle. This grew louder and louder until, around a mile from home, I felt that I had to pull over and check if there was anything noticeably wrong. I parked up and looked at the tyre which was at full pressure. In common with the other wheels the hub caps were held in place with cable ties (this was urban east London after all).

At that point, to avoid any unnecessary delay, I walked back to the church on foot in order to see whether anyone might lend me a car to be able to get to Oakington. I was lent a Nissan Micra and a welcome companion. We set off and made our visit.

The following day I returned to my car, parked-up a mile from home, and called the AA. Their roadside engineer cut the cable tie holding the rear hub cap in place and jacked the car up, whereupon the wheel fell off. It had been held in place by maybe just a simple half-turn of the nuts on each of the four bolts. Whoever had done this had then carefully replaced the hub cap and secured it with a new but differently coloured cable tie. Had I managed to get as far as the M11 two miles from home and then accelerated to a greater speed, it is likely that the wheel would have come off and the car would have veered out of control. The best outcome might have been severe damage to the vehicle.

Was this the next stage after the tyres? It does seem very strange but the problem with punctures ceased and this happened next. I find it very difficult to conceive that anyone would dislike me or my family to that extent. Perhaps it wasn't us personally. Perhaps it was something that we represented: a happy family? Mild prosperity? Possibly my role within the church? The last thing I would want to believe is that someone might have risked hurting me or my family and others seriously. We don't have religious persecution in this country; or at least we don't persecute Christians, whatever the crazy fringe might say.

Is there any more? Well yes, and in its way it has an almost comic flavour. Not too long after all this I was questioned by the police. The funny side of it (to me at least - I have a very strange sense of humour) was that the detective had the kind of accent and mode of speech reminiscent of London policemen from every Ealing comedy. His opening line of questioning also brought a smile: 'Now sir, I understand that you are some kind of reverend?'

It seems that someone had accused me of going to a certain house - I was not allowed to know which one - and demanding to get in. When the person who lived there had denied me entry, it seemed that I had attacked them, pushed past them into the house and refused to leave until they threatened to call the police to arrest me.

The policeman asked if I could explain where I was on the day in question. I was puzzled by the ridiculousness of the situation. I looked for my diary and then (with a quick and sincere prayer of thanks) was able to produce my passport, with entry and exit stamps that showed that on the day in question I was 4,000 miles away in the Pakistani city of Karachi. Which is quite an alibi when you think about it. 'I must say that didn't seem very likely, sir, that you would do this,' said the Ealing comedy policeman. 'Not with you being some kind of reverend.'

I admit that I have had fun recounting that last incident and the ridiculousness of the accusation. I am not someone who God has equipped to be a burglar or a fighter, whatever else I may be. Also the strange, exaggerated voice of the police officer that made me struggle to keep a straight face, and the crushing proof of my alibi. And, yes, I admit that there may have been some in my congregation at that time who would have loved to question how much of a 'reverend' I really was. But then the humour fades…

These three incidents are not funny at all, but rather very serious. Who are you? Why did you hate me or us so much that you acted with such malicious intent? As a person - as the target of three attacks like this - I have many questions. With the insight that sometimes comes with being a pastor, all I feel is your seething rage as a sign of deep hurt.

So, whoever you are, Tony, Lisa, Ahmed or Saira: I don't know your identity. I don't know what I did, or what you thought I did, or failed to do. Whatever it was about me or my family that provoked you so much, I hope you have moved on from it. I hope you have now found some peace. I wish you could have chosen a different way to express your emotions and maybe to have a conversation. In my experience, anger never really disappears until the root problem is exposed and solved.

Lastly, just to be clear, this was not persecution. I have been humbled to be in contact with others in parts of the world where persecution is a real and constant danger. This was just a nuisance.

* * ♦ * *

You're familiar with the old written law, 'Love your friend,' and its unwritten companion, 'Hate your enemy.' I'm challenging that. I'm telling you to love your enemies. Let them bring out the best in you, not the worst. When someone gives you a hard time, respond with the supple moves of prayer, for then you are working out of your true selves, your God-created selves. This is what God does. He gives his best—the sun to warm and the rain to nourish—to everyone, regardless: the good and bad, the nice and nasty. If all you do is love the lovable, do you expect a bonus? Anybody can do that. If you simply say hello to those who greet you, do you expect a medal? Any run-of-the-mill sinner does that. Matthew 5: 43-48

This. Just this.

YOU

"Time's up. The Son of Man is about to be betrayed into the hands of sinners. Get up. Let's get going. My betrayer has arrived." No sooner were the words out of his mouth when Judas, the one out of the Twelve, showed up, and with him a bunch of thugs, sent by the high priests, religion scholars, and leaders, brandishing swords and clubs. The betrayer had worked out a signal with them: "The one I kiss, that's the one—seize him. Make sure he doesn't get away." He went straight to Jesus and said, "Rabbi!" and kissed him. The others then grabbed him and roughed him up.

One of the men standing there unsheathed his sword, swung, and came down on the Chief Priest's servant, lopping off the man's ear. Jesus said to them, "What is this, coming after me with swords and clubs as if I were a dangerous criminal? Day after day I've been sitting in the Temple teaching, and you never so much as lifted a hand against me. What you in fact have done is confirm the prophetic writings." All the disciples bailed on him.

A young man was following along. All he had on was a bedsheet. Some of the men grabbed him but he got away, running off naked, leaving them holding the sheet. They led Jesus to the Chief Priest.
Mark 14: 43-53

Suddenly, in one moment, everything changes. Everything we have learned about you; everything we have witnessed; everything we have listened to until this point in your story stops abruptly. Before this, you are the one who drives the story forward. You travel, moving from one place to another. Your words and actions are what everyone pays attention to, including us. Everyone who meets you is transformed: they are either inspired, joyful, healed or filled with rage and hatred. Fishermen leave their nets behind. Beggars on the roadside jump to their feet. Opponents are silenced. Storms are calmed. A crowd of hungry people enjoy a satisfying meal. A dead girl comes back to life.

But then…from this point, when the guards in the garden take you away, we no longer see anything from your perspective. Suddenly you stop being the one who does things. From now on, you become the one who is done to by others, who act on you.

How can I hope in God now? For here we see one who is powerless against brutal hatred. This contradicts the image of God that I hold on to - an image that shapes my faith, my understanding and my prayers. If I believe in a God who can leap tall buildings at one bound; who is faster than a speeding bullet; who sees all that is hidden, then I pray expecting you to behave that way. To be honest, that is the naive image of God that I usually have in my mind. Naive, because I stick to that image even when you do not act like Superman. But here, in the gospel story, I am asked to think of you as vulnerable. You are no longer active in this story of yours. You are no longer speaking, teaching, healing or casting out. No, no. From this point on, you have been given over to the control of others; abused and tortured; brought before weak politicians and seething religious leaders and exposed to public shame.

* * ♦ * *

It seems that I have to accept both images of God as powerful and supernatural, and as vulnerable and human, because they are both found in the Bible. I cannot just pick one image that I like and ignore the other one that I find unsettling and disappointing. Maybe a bit frightening too.

Several years ago, and in another place, I experienced two distinct illustrations of how people of faith behave when confronted with the vulnerability of Christ and the abandonment of God. The first was a truly moving experience for me when, as a guest in an Anglican congregation on Maundy Thursday, I watched the ritual that is the stripping of the altar. All decoration and ornamentation is removed, piece by piece, until everything is left empty and lifeless ready for the next day's Good Friday service. I cannot describe the feeling of grief and loss in that simple act. It is an acknowledgement that Christ is going to die. That God loves his creation so much that, having become human and lived among us, he dies. At that moment, I can begin to grasp a little of what it must have been for those who first loved you and followed you to watch your tortured body die.

The second experience was also on Maundy Thursday, this time in a very packed hall where, after communion, the congregation was asked to leave quietly so that, in some small way, we would be able to feel the forsakenness of Christ and the betrayal of his friends. As the people slowly walked to the doors in a silence that was different from our usual joyful worship, the shock of the death of God became too hard for some. They could not handle it at all. So, on the night Jesus was given over to his foes, they started singing a victorious Easter Day song. It was one of the most disturbing and unsettling church experiences I have had. To believe in the resurrection means we have to believe that Christ died. His heart stopped beating. He had no brain activity. On Good Friday and on the day after, God is dead.

Some Christians think (though they might not admit it), that the only three days in your life, Jesus, that really count are those between the first Good Friday and Easter Day. For them, the previous 33 years of your life were just a long preamble to the main event. For it was only in those three days, they believe, that you secured our salvation. Your birth, life, death and burial are just a warm-up in the rush to resurrection. I no longer believe that. I think we learn as much from your life as from your death: a human being who was born to be one of us. We call this your incarnation, meaning to become flesh or to be embodied:

The Word became flesh and blood and moved into the neighbourhood. John 1:14

You have made your home among us, wherever we are.

And then this:

Think of yourselves the way Christ Jesus thought of himself. He had equal status with God but didn't think so much of himself that he had to cling to the advantages of that status no matter what. Not at all. When the time came, he set aside the privileges of deity and took on the status of a slave, became human! Having become human, he stayed human. It was an incredibly humbling process. He didn't claim special privileges. Instead, he lived a selfless, obedient life and then died a selfless, obedient death—and the worst kind of death at that—a crucifixion. Philippians 2: 5-8

You chose to identify with all people. You decided to be like us. You were born in a region far from the major centres of power, into a world that is chaotic, full of danger, oppression and fear. You would feel comfortable in Southend-on-Sea or London or Kyiv or Karachi or anywhere, really. You have lived through the situations, limitations, struggles and doubts that all humans face, some more than others.

You were not born fully grown but went through the pain and vulnerability of childbirth. Your first years were reliant on your parents and others. To put it plainly, you - the eternal Second Person of the Trinity - needed your bottom cleaned and your nappy changed several times a day.

You lacked knowledge. The Word, by whose voice everything that exists was made, needed to learn language, vocabulary, awareness and fine motor skills. Gradually, naturally, your physical and spiritual growth started to happen. You grew socially, showing clearly that the spiritual and social aspects of a person are not separate but connected to the physical. This is the 're-enactment' by God of human experience. You ate, drank, played, worshipped, loved, read, worked, washed and bled. You went to the toilet. Your vulnerability - the frailty of humanity - is part of being Immanuel: God with us.

Now, having pushed aside a false image of you as Superman, please don't allow us to favour just one biblical image of God over another. We are left with the paradox that you are also God. But how might we now see you if our prayers for healing from sickness or disability or mental illness or poverty have not yet been answered? And we - who want to make your story the one by which we live – how do we reflect this image of you?

For three hundred years after these events, the church was the 'done-to': on the margins of society; distrusted; resisted and persecuted. In its seeming weakness, that church was strong because - however imperfectly it grew in different contexts - it stayed close to your character and values. When we, your followers, show your vulnerability, we are at our strongest. When we try to be strong - to be influential and powerful in society or to have control - we risk losing the very values for which you lived and died.

We see this in all sorts of ways. I sometimes encounter Christians who long for Britain to become 'once again' a Christian country. Now I understand their desire to live in a place where you are honoured, but I don't believe that there has ever been or could be a Christian country. That is to miss the point.[ix] When Christians do not seek your vulnerability, they search for proxy leaders: Trump at the large scale; or church pastors as cult heroes at the local.

We pray for revival, though the revival so many Christians seek so often requires you to deliver what they would like – a repeat of what you have done before rather than the heart's desire of the one who says *'Look! I'm making everything new!'*

Why is any of this relevant to us? Jesus, in speaking to your disciples you said: *'I am sending you out as sheep among wolves.'* You never intended that we should be fierce, strong or predatory. We are to take nothing with us and to depend upon others. To share in your vulnerability and to know your strength, which is shown perfectly in our weakness.

This book has been a collection of tales, not of the strong or famous or accomplished. Instead, it has been the unfamiliar stories of those who have not yet inherited the earth. It is in their frailty and vulnerability and their lack of wider recognition that we may catch a glimpse of you. You imagined each one of them as a unique and treasured person and you lived a life, most of which was spent mundanely, just like us. In an age that worships celebrity, we do not find you among the celebrated but among the ignored and the meek.

I love the way James Allan Francis described you in *One solitary life:*

Here is a man who was born in an obscure village, the child of a peasant woman. He grew up in another obscure village, where He worked in a carpenter shop until He was thirty, and then for three years He was an itinerant preacher.

He never wrote a book. He never held an office. He never owned a home. He never had a family. He never went to college. He never put his foot inside a big city. He never traveled two hundred miles from the place where He was born. He never did one of the things that usually accompany greatness. He had no credentials but Himself. He had nothing to do with this world except the naked power of His divine manhood.

While still a young man, the tide of public opinion turned against Him. His friends ran away. One of them denied Him. He was turned over to His enemies. He went through the mockery of a trial. He was nailed to a cross between two thieves. His executioners gambled for the only piece of property He had on earth while He was dying—and that was his coat. When he was dead He was taken down and laid in a borrowed grave through the pity of a friend.

Nineteen wide centuries have come and gone and today He is the centrepiece of the human race and the leader of the column of progress. I am far within the mark when I say that all the armies that ever marched, and all the navies that ever were built, and all the parliaments that ever sat, all the kings that ever reigned, put together have not affected the life of man upon this earth as powerfully as has that One Solitary Life.[x]

* * ♦ * *

LOVE

"Would you know your Lord's meaning in this thing?
Know it well: Love was his meaning.
Who showed it to you? Love.
What did He show you? Love.
Why did He show it? For love." [xi]

So now the stories have now been told and my friends have been named and honoured. You will have noticed that Christ is the thread that runs through all these tales. I name him as the constant in my own story also. Somehow, I have been written into a bigger story that is being told right now by a greater Storyteller than me. How does that feel? It is like having glimpses of an elusive but constant Love gazing at me. This Love has pursued me doggedly, in different times and places, in easier times and harder; sometimes alone but often in the company of others. It is by grace alone that I ever catch a glimpse of this Love, through the smoke of foolishness and self-absorption that so often clouds my vision.

I first felt this Love as a child and it has recurred in every stage of my life. I am grateful to those who spoke of it: in the Boys' Brigade; in many churches and among fellow Christians; in daily life yet often catching me by surprise. For friends, whose own experiences bless me. This Love – by which of course I mean the God-who-is-love - only desires that I should allow him to transform me so that I become loving, like him.

This Love is not soft or vague or indulgent: it is much harder than that. For this Love is also Truth. It doesn't let me get away with my lies or compromises.

This Love has a name: Jesus. He told his friends that God is like a treasure hidden in a field that someone finds and then sells everything else to buy that field and own that treasure.[xii] *Everything.* Anything I insist on bringing with me is just a distraction. I must rediscover the value of everything by returning again and again to the place of responding to that Love.

Now there are many days when I don't feel or glimpse anything. But, ultimately, only this infinite Love truly has meaning for me. He is the God who reaches out to each of us, longing for and accepting us. The transformation he promises and desires begins whenever we respond to that Love. And so the story continues …

> On gravelly beach
> I catch the glint of sea-glass in
> Green and blue and frosted white
> Each shard precious in the moment
> And still each various day
> Twice-washed, snatching my gaze
> Shining back and piercing me in its radiance.

I lie there also, anchored in
Rough, cold, granular grind
Estuary essence
Vitreous edges slicing
Sharpened speck, churned in aggregate sweep
Sheering, exposing planes
To be ground
Before immersion once again under
Lumpen brown-grey.

Now shattered
Scattered
Unable to be
What once was purposed.
Then wave-hewn anew,
Sunken, I lie lost
Waiting to be sea-sifted and
Treasured for what I am
And shall become. [xiii]

* * ♦ * *

NOTES, REFERENCES, THANKS AND ABOUT THE AUTHOR

The story of Bruno is taken from a memorial address for Jean Bruno Mbou, which was delivered at Cranbrook Baptist Church, Ilford on 20 November 2010.

The letter that begins the chapter on Fred and Don is the text of a genuine letter sent on VE Day 1945 from my uncle, Fred James, to his youngest half-brother, my father Donald King.

The reflection entitled 'You' is greatly influenced by Canon W H Vanstone's *The Stature of Waiting* (London: Darton, Longman & Todd Ltd; new edition, 2004). In the 1980s I was privileged to hear Canon Vanstone speaking, drawing on his other major work entitled *'Love's endeavour, love's expense'*. He was a gifted but humble man who rejected career progression within the church in order to remain a parish priest, writer and thinker. We need more like him.

Thanks

I am grateful to the two churches that have allowed me to serve them in ministry and leadership: Cranbrook Baptist Church in Ilford and Church from

Scratch in Southend-on-Sea. Also those churches that have welcomed me as a regular friend, speaker and contributor over the past 40 years.

Thanks are also due to Baptists Together for allowing me compassionate leave when I needed it and for then kindly agreeing that I should remain on the active list of accredited ministers, with a portfolio role. Among other things, this has given me the space to reflect and write this book.

My sincere thanks go to Rev'd Lynn Green and Bishop John Perumbalath for so kindly reviewing this book and offering their commendations.

Does anyone really read the lists of names in acknowledgements unless you hope (or fear) that your name will appear therein? In which case, I hope the following friends read my heartfelt thanks for reading and commenting upon drafts or for their steadfast encouragement: Ashley and Rachel, Rich, Andy and Anthony. To John, for your continuing partnership in prayer. My sister Avril kindly agreed to the inclusion of Uncle Fred's letter to Dad. Both Nikki and Ethan offered their critically supportive comments on aspects of the book as I wrote. Thank you all.

About me

I am a Baptist Minister and charity consultant. Born in south London, I and my family have lived in Southend-on-Sea in Essex since 2009. I enjoy books, quiet pubs, dogs and conversation with friends. One of my hobbies is oral storytelling, sharing stories of both faith and folklore. 2024 marks my 40th anniversary as a preacher.

I have chosen to use both of my Christian names for this book because, perhaps surprisingly, across the wide world there are more people who share my name than I imagined, including at least one who has published in a Christian context.

* * ♦ * *

References

---

[i] With apologies to Kierkegaard for re-ordering his quotation. The more usual translation of the original reads: 'Life can only be understood backwards, but it must be lived forwards.' The source is: Søren Kierkegaard, *Journalen* JJ:167 (1843), *Søren Kierkegaards Skrifter*, Søren Kierkegaard Research Center, Copenhagen, 1997, volume 18, page 306

[ii] William Barclay, The Gospel of Luke, (London: Westminster Press, 1953)

[iii] Gerard Manley Hopkins, Poems and prose, (London: Penguin Classics; Reprint edition, 2008), page 12

[iv] Book of Common Prayer, 2nd edition, (Cambridge: Cambridge University Press, 2004)

[v] Karl Barth made this point before me. He knew a thing or two.

[vi] Composed by the author.

[vii] Margery Kempe (author) and B A Windeatt (translator), The Book of Margery Kempe, (Penguin Classics), Revised edition October 1985

[viii] Professor C E M Joad: This man, anti-God for most of his life, shocked the British scientific community by displaying all the characteristics of a Damascus Road experience and preaching the truths he once lived to deny. This quotation was given in the BBC Brains Trust programme.

[ix] I think such a concept is a category error. A helpful guide to this topic, albeit in a US context, is Gregory Boyd, The Myth of a Christian Nation: how the quest for political power is destroying the church, (Zondervan, 2009)

[x] Usually attributed to Revd James Allan Francis, *One Solitary Life,* pp. 1–7 (1963), originally delivered as a sermon on 11 July 1926 to the Baptist Young People's Union at a Los Angeles Convention.

[xi] Julian of Norwich (author) and Barry Windeatt (translator), *Revelations of divine love,* Oxford: OUP, 2015, chapter 86

[xii] Matthew 13:44

[xiii] Composed by the author.

Printed in Great Britain
by Amazon